Chicken Soup for the Teenage Soul
The Real Deal: CHALLENGES

Chicken Soup for the Teenage Soul

The Real Deal: CHALLENGES

Stories about Disses, Losses Messes, Stresses & More

Jack Canfield
Mark Victor Hansen
Deborah Reber

Health Communications, Inc.
Deerfield Beach, Florida

www.hcibooks.com
www.chickensoup.com

Library of Congress Cataloging-in-Publication Data
is on file with the Library of Congress.

© 2006 John T. Canfield and Hansen and Hansen LLC
ISBN-13: 978-0-7573-0407-1
ISBN-10: 0-7573-0407-9

Publisher: Health Communications, Inc.
          3201 S.W. 15th Street
          Deerfield Beach, FL 33442–8190

Cover photos ©BananaStock, ©Shutterstock, ©Rubberball Productions
Cover and inside book design by Lawna Patterson Oldfield

CONTENTS

CHAPTER 3 **Family Affairs**

CHAPTER 4 **Losing It**

CHAPTER 5 **Stabbed in the Back**

CHAPTER 6 What's Happening Out There?

CHAPTER 7 Pressure

CHAPTER 8 Finding Your Voice

INTRODUCTION

CHALLENGES. We all have them. Big ones, little ones, seemingly insurmountable ones. They're a part of *everyone's* life. It may seem like some people have more challenging lives than others, and while this may be true, it's not how many challenges you have or how intense they are that matters—it's about how you deal with the challenges that come your way.

They say that you can never know what someone else's life is like until you've walked a mile in their shoes. Well, I think that's true. Everyone has their own thing going on. We're all unique— from our DNA and our upbringing and home life to our way of looking at the world. And what might be no big deal for one person might be a huge challenge for someone else, and vice versa.

Challenges don't have to be the end of the world (and it's a good thing, too, or the world would have ended a long time ago). With the right perspective and the right tools, we can get through life's challenges in style. We might even come out the other side of a challenge in better shape than we were before the challenge arose. Don't believe me? Well, I have an example that might change your thinking. Ever heard of Lance Armstrong? At the top of his game, cyclist Lance Armstrong was faced with a huge challenge—he was diagnosed with widespread cancer and given less than a 50 percent chance of surviving. But not only did Lance Armstrong survive, he came back to make sports history by winning the grueling Tour de France a record six times in a row and making his mark as one of the most gifted athletes of all time.

While this is a pretty extreme example, the moral of the story is one worth remembering. Even when challenges seem like more than we can take, we *can* face them, and we *can* overcome them. And that's where this book comes in. In the pages of this book are real stories and real poems from teens like you—teens who are facing challenges like eating disorders and broken families and natural disasters and low self-esteem. Woven in among these moving stories and poems are tons of sidebars on everything from movies to see and books to read, to ideas for handling your own challenges and quizzes to help you figure out where you stand when it comes to tough issues. And just like the other *Real Deal* books, you'll get my point of view throughout too, as I write introductions to each teen-written contribution. And who am I, you ask? My name is Deborah Reber, and I'm a writer living in Seattle with a special interest in working with teens. Why? Because I used to be one, and I know how difficult it can be.

We've worked hard to put this book together for you, and we hope that it becomes a handbook to help you get through the curveballs that life throws you. We hope that no matter what your challenges are, you can see your experiences through the words in this book and discover useful strategies for coming out on top.

Deborah Reber

ACKNOWLEDGMENTS

THE PATH TO *Chicken Soup for the Teenage Soul The Real Deal: Challenges* has been a challenging and re-warding one. Our heartfelt gratitude to:

Our families, who have been chicken soup for our souls!

Jack's family, Inga, Travis, Riley, Christopher, Oran and Kyle, for all their love and support.

Mark's family, Patty, Elisabeth and Melanie, for once again sharing and lovingly supporting us in creating yet another book.

Deborah's husband Derin and son Asher, for sharing their love, energy and encouragement with us every day, as well as Dale, MaryLou and Michele Reber, and David and Barbara Basden for their ongoing support.

Our publisher, Peter Vegso, for his vision and commitment to bringing *Chicken Soup for the Soul* to the world.

Patty Aubery and Russ Kalmaski, for being there on every step of the journey, with love, laughter and endless creativity.

Barbara LoMonaco, for nourishing us with truly wonderful stories.

D'ette Corona for her incredible powers of organization and securing all the permissions and bios for this book.

Patty Hansen, for her thorough and competent handling of the legal and licensing aspects of the *Chicken Soup for the Soul* books. You are magnificent at the challenge!

Laurie Hartman, for being a precious guardian of the *Chicken Soup* brand.

Veronica Romero, Teresa Esparza, Robin Yerian, Jesse Ianniello, Lauren Edelstein, Patti Clement, Maegan Romanello, Cassidy Guyer, Noelle Champagne, Jody Emme, Debbie Lefever, Michelle Adams, Dee Dee Romanello, Shanna Vieyra, and Gina Romanello who support Jack's and Mark's businesses with skill and love.

Our appreciation to Bret Witter for his suggestions and guidance during the development of the manuscript.

Michele Matrisciani, Allison Janse, Andrea Gold and Kathy Grant, our editors at Health Communications, Inc., for their devotion to excellence.

Terry Burke, Tom Sand, Lori Golden, Kelly Johnson Maragni, Patricia McConnell, Kim Weiss, Paola Fernandez-Rana and Julie de la Cruz—the marketing, sales and PR departments at Health Communications, Inc., for doing such an incredible job supporting our books.

Tom Sand, Claude Choquette and Luc Jutras, who manage year after year to get our books translated into thirty-six languages around the world.

The art department at Health Communications, Inc., for their talent, creativity and unrelenting patience in producing book covers and inside designs that capture the essence of *Chicken Soup*: Larissa Hise Henoch, Lawna Patterson Oldfield,

Andrea Perrine Brower, Anthony Clausi, Kevin Stawieray and Dawn Von Strolley Grove.

All of the *Chicken Soup for the Soul* coauthors, who make it such a joy to be part of this *Chicken Soup* family.

Deborah's intern, Anna Minard, for sharing her excellent research skills and proofreading the first draft.

Our readers who helped us make the final selections and made invaluable suggestions on how to improve the book, including Ed Adams, Tipton Blish, Julie Johnson, AnneMarie Kane, Jamie Koelln, Bridget Perry, Renee Zak and Alice Wilder.

WriteGirl (*www.writegirl.org*), New Moon Publications (*www.newmoon.org*), Write On (*www.zest.net/writeon*), About Creative Writing for Teens (*www.teenwriting.about.com*) and Crai Bower for reaching out to teens in the search for submissions.

And, most of all, to everyone who submitted their heartfelt stories and poems for possible inclusion in this book. While we were not able to use everything you sent in, we know that each word came from a magical place flourishing within your soul.

Because of the size of this project, we may have left out the names of some people who contributed along the way. If so, we are sorry, but please know that we really do appreciate you very much.

We are truly grateful and love you all!

CHAPTER 1

EMOTIONAL BASKET CASE

Have you ever just felt like you couldn't handle what's coming your way? Like your emotions were spiraling out of control and you were powerless to do anything about it? When you feel this way, it's easy to think you're completely alone and that no one else could or will ever understand what it's like to be you. But take solace . . . everyone feels this way at some point or another. They just handle it in different ways. This chapter deals with being an emotional basket case, and gives some strategies for reining those emotions back in.

HOW COOL WOULD IT BE IF every time we were feeling confused or frustrated or heartbroken or so angry that we couldn't see straight, we could just flip a switch and sound the alarm? The brigade would come running, armed with whatever we needed—tissues, Chunky Monkey ice cream, an older sibling to set things straight. Unfortunately, there is no such switch. In fact, many of us aren't very good at letting others know what's really going on with us, or knowing how good it would be for us if we could.

When I used to get upset, I'd withdraw into my own little world, letting only my dog in for comfort, probably because he was the only one I knew who wouldn't talk back and would love me no matter what I was feeling. And even though once the secret was out, my friends and family always came through, putting my thoughts and fears out there was a scary thing. The author of this next poem is grappling with the same issue, and has found an outlet for her hidden emotions through her pen and the power of words.

Silent Scream

Outside, you see me smiling
And floating through each day,
A little tired, a little thin,
But overall, okay.

But you don't hear my anguished
   thoughts
Which surface every night.
They plague me, haunt me, torment me
'Til I'm too weak to fight.

CONSIDER THIS . . .

Even people who **seem to have it all** can be **secretly** living in a world of pain. Actress Brooke Shields revealed her own struggle with **depression** following the birth of her baby in the book *Down Came the Rain* (2005).

And so, next day, I come to
   school
With deeply shadowed eyes.
I smile, laugh and speak on
   cue,
Living a pack of lies.

A silent scream echoes inside,
Reaction to my lie—
'Til with no warning, it erupts
And I crumble down and cry.

Come find me, help me, make it stop—
No! Keep out, go away!
For if you come, I've no control
Over the words I say.

Can't you hear my silent scream,
Decipher what I hide?
So come and ask me what is wrong,
Come sit down by my side.

If nothing else, then please read
   through
This tangled web I weave.
For you are really not the one
I'm trying to deceive.

Help me—I don't know what I want
I've lost my guiding light.
Please hold me, let me cry and say
Somehow, you'll make it right.

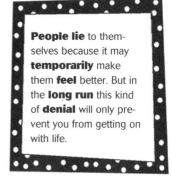

HOW ABOUT YOU?

Have you ever **felt** like the **life** you're living is a **lie?** How do you deal?

CONSIDER THIS . . .

People lie to themselves because it may **temporarily** make them **feel** better. But in the **long run** this kind of **denial** will only prevent you from getting on with life.

Perhaps, deep down, I know what's wrong,
What keeps me up awake.
What is the source of all my tears
And ever-there heartache.

But not yet can I face it,
Or maybe I just won't.
Please, someone, help me understand—
God only knows I don't.

Ashley Yang, Age 16

OUTSIDE THE BOX

Feeling confused or depressed? Emotions like this can spiral out of control if we don't find a way to face them. Here are some thoughts to take to heart:

- Take care of yourself! Do the things that make you feel good, like exercising or hanging out with friends.
- Talk to someone you trust and let them know how you feel. It might be hard to do, but depression needs to be taken very seriously.
- Be patient and don't expect quick fixes. Depression can sometimes take a while to get over.

Spotlight On ... DEPRESSION

You may hear people say that they feel "depressed," but is that what's *really* going on? The experts say there's a difference between being "depressed" and feeling down. While you may feel blue occasionally, in general people who are "down" can cope with day-to-day life, even if they aren't as happy as they think they should be. Depression, on the other hand, is an illness that affects the way a person thinks and feels about everything. People who are clinically depressed might experience symptoms like feeling sad and hopeless, losing their energy, having no appetite and finding it difficult to concentrate.

And while most people experience times when they feel down or sad, fewer than one in five people ever experience serious clinical depression. Those who suffer from depression can come from all walks of life: rich, poor, male, female, young and old.

Depression is a serious illness, but there are many different kinds of treatment available, including therapy and/or certain medications. People can be cured from their depression or discover coping techniques that can help them get through rough patches. But depression shouldn't be handled alone—talking to someone and getting help is just about the best thing any depressed person can do.

For more information about depression, check out iFred, the International Foundation for Research and Education on Depression, at *www.ifred.org*.

IF YOU'VE EVER SEEN A CLASSIC JAILHOUSE MOVIE like *The Shawshank Redemption*, you know that some prisoners are deemed so bad and disruptive that they're placed in solitary confinement. For days, weeks . . . even months, these prisoners are kept isolated from the rest of the world. Sound tough? It is. Solitary confinement is considered the harshest of punishments because it's so mentally difficult to deal with.

So it's no wonder that if you've ever felt isolated, the emotions that go along with it are pretty intense. And even though isolation is technically defined as being "separated and apart from others," that's not always the case. Sometimes we can feel isolated even when surrounded by thousands of people. Like the author of the poem "Left Behind" writes, sometimes isolation arises when we think no one understands what we're going through, where we are or how we feel.

CONSIDER THIS . . .

Some of the effects of **solitary confinement** include things like:
• hallucinations
• memory loss
• identity loss
• difficulty concentrating
• anxiety
• uncontrollable crying

Left Behind

A beautiful girl sits at the computer
    and stares,
    Waiting by herself for someone to care.
    No messages pop up, no one calls her
    phone,
        Life passes her by as she sits home
        alone.

Her heart hurts with emptiness, there's nothing inside.
She just needs a friend in whom she can confide.
She wishes things were different, the way they used to be,
When she mattered to people, or so it seemed.

Those people she thought would be her best friends forever?
At the first sign of change did what they said they would never.
They found new friends and didn't need her anymore.
But change is change—all is fair in love and war.

She still loves them now even if they're gone,
It's a shame she's the only one who
    wasn't able to move on.
She can burst any second, the
    tears are so hard to fight,
She puts on an act at school and
    cries herself to sleep at night.

She's at her lowest point but
    refuses to break,
And continues to live the life that's
    so ridiculously fake.

CONSIDER THIS . . .

Where did the idea of **"happily ever after"** come from anyway? The **reality** is, life is a blend of **happy** and **sad times**, amazing times and not-so-great times. If we can find a way to **appreciate the good times**, the low times won't seem as bad.

She's living in the past, remembering
     days full of laughter,
So whatever happened to living
     happily ever after?

         Maurisa Cohen, Age 16

OUTSIDE THE BOX

Do you ever feel isolated, like no one understands what's going on with you? Here are some ideas for coming out of your self-imposed solitary confinement:

- Make regular plans with a friend once a week. Even if the last thing you feel like doing is getting out of the house, a change of scenery and the distraction of friend-time will do you a world of good.
- Figure out what you're saying to yourself that's making you feel isolated. Write your thoughts down and then challenge each and every one of them.
- Get involved in something that you enjoy— sports, tap dancing, the debate team. When you're doing something that makes you feel good, your feelings of isolation will be overshadowed by the activity.

I'M THE FIRST PERSON TO SAY that believing in a little magic can be a great thing. Think about it . . . so many of the great artists and philosophers and musicians and scholars made their marks through believing in the magic of their abilities . . . through *dreaming big*.

But can believing in something fantastical ever be a *bad* thing? I think so, especially when magical things or fantasies take the place of reality. Life can sometimes be hard to handle, especially when the plot deviates from what you might read in a classic fairy tale.

 Read It?

In *Freaky Green Eyes* by Joyce Carol Oates, main character Franky spends much of her time **living in denial** about her **father's abuse** of her mother.

Saying Good-Bye to Fairy Tales

I really don't know how or when my view on fairy tales changed. I grew up a naïve, young girl, head full of stories involving handsome princes and happy endings. I held on to the notion that a handsome prince would ride up on his big white horse and rescue me from the cold, cruel world.

As I entered high school, my naïve heart fell helplessly for any "handsome prince" that happened to glance my way. I so desperately

For Real?

Fairy tales are a kind of "folk" tale, meaning they have been passed down from generation to generation. They were not originally intended for children at all. In fact, fairy tales were often gruesome and scary, and were meant to teach lessons to adults who were in trouble with the law.

wanted to feel the magic of love that I convinced myself every crush was "the one." Although time and time again my poor heart was left disappointed, I remained stubborn and determined. I was foolishly convinced that my fairy tale would come true if I just kept believing.

Seen It?

In *Ella Enchanted* (2004), a fairy tale with a twist, Ella has a spell cast upon her to always be obedient, something that gets her in trouble when bad people take advantage of her.

Then, somewhere along the way, everything changed. I experienced heartbreak—the worst kind imaginable. The innocence I had held onto for seventeen years was suddenly snatched out from under me. The pain I felt inside was so strong, I wouldn't wish it on anyone, not even my worst enemy. Suddenly, my fantasy-filled world evaporated, leaving me cold, alone and scared. This time, there was no prince to come to my rescue. There was only me and my newly damaged soul.

That's when I became "tough." I stopped caring about everyone, most importantly myself. Somehow, my once compassionate heart became cold. Subconsciously, I wanted to hurt those around me. I lashed out at my friends, my family . . . everyone I loved. On the outside, I appeared careless and cold, but on the inside, I was dying. I thought it was unfair that I was in so much pain, while those around me felt nothing. I was angry at others for not realizing what I was going through. But how were they to know?

HOW ABOUT YOU?

Do you think **you** have unrealistic expectations about the way your relationships and friendships **should** work out?

I kept pushing and pushing, and eventually, I pushed so hard that I snapped. Finally, I broke down and recognized what was going on inside of me. Once I faced my pain, I could finally begin the healing process. Almost a year later, I am able to sit here and write this as a changed person. I've watched the deep wounds inflicted upon my soul slowly fade to scars.

As I pieced my broken heart back together, I realize how much my life has changed. I am no longer the naïve dreamer I once was, nor am I the bitter, damaged girl I was after my heartbreak. Slowly, I am regaining the ability to feel again—to love, to trust. Most importantly, I am learning to respect and love *myself* again. The pain of my past has made me a stronger person, and from that I have found the strength to finally leave the past where it belongs . . . in the past.

Andrea Popp, Age 18

OUTSIDE THE BOX

Going through a painful heartbreak? Here are some creative ways to spark the healing process:

- <u>Write!</u> Write down everything you want to say to the person who hurt you. Get the thoughts out of your head and down onto paper.
- <u>Talk!</u> Talk to a close friend or family member about how you're feeling.
- <u>Distract!</u> Watch movies that you love, go for long walks, sleep over at a friend's house, read a good book.
- <u>Be kind to yourself!</u> Give yourself time to get over the pain and believe that you will eventually go back to feeling like you, because you will.

HAVE YOU EVER HEARD OF A "SELF-FULFILLING PROPHECY"? That's the whole idea that if we tell ourselves something is going to happen enough times, then we can actually make it happen. For example, say you have a friend who is convinced she's going to fall flat on her face when she walks up to the podium during a school assembly. If she focuses on how terrible it would be if she actually did wipe out, she can actually *make* it happen because that's all she's been focusing on.

I used to go through life like this, waiting for the other shoe to drop. But then I learned to chill out and not worry so much. I realized that there are some things that are just out of my control, and that stuff's going to happen, good and bad, whether I worry or not. So I ask you this—is it really worth it to stress over things that are out of our control?

Thin Ice

With each small step
the ice cracks below.
Walking forward,
the crevice widens.
I slip and slide,
arms thrown out
to catch the fall.
A scream in my throat,
ready to release,
but nothing comes out.
I see the moment outside myself,
and yet my nerves can feel it.

For Real?

3–4 inches is the minimum depth for ice to **safely** hold one person **without breaking**.

CONSIDER THIS . . .

The sound of breaking ice
like thunder, gunshots,
   screams and bombs
in the once-silent dead of
   night.
My breath stops short.
I gasp for air
but only get water,
like frozen liquid steel
coating my insides.
I'm in over my head!

Some people who **study dreams** say that anxiety dreams are actually **healthy** ways to **release** pent-up **stress**, and that many people have the exact same dreams. Here are some of the more common themes in anxiety dreams:

• Falling
• Being late for a test
• Moving in slow motion
• Getting caught naked in public
• Drowning

I jolt awake.
My clothes stick to my sweating body.
My skin is cold and clammy,
but I feel as though I have just raced through
the deepest, hottest fires of hell.
My heart thumps to the beat of panic.
My premonitions frighten me.
It hasn't happened yet,
but I know it will.
I cradle my head in my hands
   and cry.
Others have crossed the stream,
but I'm the one on thin ice.

Teresa Rankin, Age 19

HOW ABOUT YOU?

Have you ever had an **"anxiety dream"**?

WHERE DO YOU STAND?

Do you create self-fulfilling prophecies?

___ YES ___ NO   You can't help replaying in your mind what happened during your last track meet when you tripped over a hurdle. You're afraid of doing the same thing at the next meet.

___ YES ___ NO   You're dying to ask your crush to go to the Spring Fling Dance, but don't know if you can do it—what if he or she says "no" and humiliates you?

___ YES ___ NO   You've been rehearsing to be the lead drummer in marching band all summer, but have a deep-rooted fear of choking in the middle of your audition.

___ YES ___ NO   Your final test in Russian History is one big essay, but you don't bother to review your notes before the test—you figure that if you haven't learned it by now, there's no way you'll retain anything new.

___ YES ___ NO   You know you're capable of hitting the high note in your chorus solo, but during the dress rehearsal your voice cracks because you shy off. Now you're sure the same thing's going to happen on the night of the show.

If you answered "yes" to more than two of these, your negative thoughts might be influencing the results you get!

I REMEMBER WHEN I WAS IN FOURTH GRADE, this new girl, Rebecca, started school in the middle of the year. Mr. Fisher introduced her to the rest of the class, and I definitely remember that the only thing running through my mind was that this poor new girl had it really tough—not only did she wear thick-rimmed glasses, but she had braces to boot. I hadn't known anyone with braces *and* glasses. *A double whammy*, I thought to myself. I think I was even more surprised when I got to know her and realized that she really wasn't any different from anyone else in my class. (I also found it ironic that by the time high school rolled around, Rebecca had perfectly straight teeth and wore contacts, while I was plagued with braces and had to wear glasses to see the blackboard.)

Looking back, I think that my friends and I must have all had things about us that we felt set us apart from the rest of our peers, things that somehow made us not fit in. And even though we were all trying to achieve it, there was no perfect standard, no true ideal. It took a back brace and a lot of soul searching for the author of this next story to learn how to let go of her desire to be just like everybody else.

Living with Scoliosis

We all have times when we feel ugly. It doesn't matter if it's due to influences from the media or comments from other people—we all suffer from issues relating to body image on some level. There are many notions of what the "perfect"

Address Book

Mind on the Media is an organization aimed at teaching teens how to think critically about the messages they see in the media about body image. For more information, check out: *www.mindon themedia.org*.

For Real?

Teens tend to become **self-conscious** right about the time their bodies start going through the physical changes of **puberty**, becoming more and more self-conscious with each passing year.

body is, it's hard to believe so much emphasis is placed on such a trivial thing. Yet, people feel pressured all the time— they're too skinny, too fat, too tall, too short. But pressure like this only promotes feelings of inadequacy and serves to make the targets of such pressure feel ugly.

When I was young, I never cared about how I looked. All I cared about was having fun with my friends, climbing trees and not letting bad things get me down. Then sixth grade came, and while I still didn't notice anything wrong with my appearance, I did start paying attention to what I wore to dances and things like that. Like every preteen, I wanted boys to like me, but I was still myself and I wasn't going to change.

But even though I wasn't paying much attention to my body, my family was. We went to a chiropractor, and as it turns out, I had scoliosis. The summer before eighth grade,

THE WORD

Scoliosis is a curvature of the spine, but instead of curving from the top to the bottom, it curves from side to side.

everything changed when I was told I needed a back brace for my scoliosis. Given only a 50-percent chance that it would help, I agreed to wear it, mainly because of family pressure. At the time I had no clue how the brace would end up affecting me, but it was decided. I would get the brace.

Seen It?

Joan Cusack plays a girl with a **scoliosis** back brace in the John Hughes' classic, *Sixteen Candles* (1984).

I started school that year with a new back brace and a brand-new rolling backpack. I was ready to lie about why I used the rolling backpack, since I knew that it stood out. *No one* could know about the brace. Baggy shirts hid the evidence, and I vowed to sit up straighter than ever before. Then PE came. My mother and I had made arrangements with the PE teacher so I could change in her office, as I needed someone to help me take the brace off and put it back on. Each day I would leave lunch early to get there before anyone else, and my teacher would, too. Sometimes I was spotted going in and out of her office, and people wondered what was going on, but I kept my lips sealed.

I managed to make friends that year, but I hardly even noticed because every day I came home and

CONSIDER THIS . . .

Rolling backpacks are gaining in popularity in schools, mostly because they take the **pressure off** of kids' **backs** when they're lugging around tons of schoolbooks.

shut myself in my room, crying for hours in the dark. I hated my baggy shirts, my unusual backpack, the wondering stares. I wanted so much for people to like me, to not feel like an outcast. I couldn't do certain things asked of me in class, and that made me want to cry, too. I felt like the ugliest person that year, with all the big clothes and huge jackets and how much it hurt to stand so straight for all those hours so no one would notice my brace. I didn't let people hug me because I couldn't let them find out. I hated how much the brace made me sweat, but there was nothing I could do about it.

CONSIDER THIS . . .

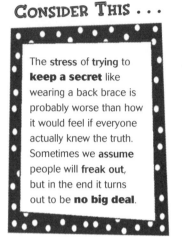

The **stress** of **trying** to **keep a secret** like wearing a back brace is probably worse than how it would feel if everyone actually knew the truth. Sometimes we **assume** people will **freak out**, but in the end it turns out to be **no big deal**.

One day in class, my cover was blown. I bent over my assignment for just a second, but it was too late. My crush saw the brace and asked, "What's that?"

My heart stopped for a second, and my instinct was to run away. Then a girl I didn't like told him it was a back brace. When class let out, I could hear them talking and laughing as I walked out the door as fast as I could, fighting back tears. When I got home the tears came rushing out—I felt humiliated and hurt. I later found out that my crush was dating that same girl who had made fun of me.

I haven't felt that ugly since that fateful day, but I still remember those feelings and how much I hated my body. But despite everything about that year, I came out of it with some great friends who have proven themselves to be true even today.

Read It?

In *The Grooming of Alice* by Phyllis Reynolds Naylor, Alice and her friends start off the summer before high school with one goal—to make their **bodies perfect**. In the end, they realize they've got to make changes on the inside, not the outside.

It saddens me that so many young girls have to suffer from comments that prey on their insecurities. I know boys can suffer just as much, too. A world that puts so much emphasis on superficial things is not a world we should have to deal with. I'm not hopeful that the degrading comments will stop, though. We are told not to judge a book by its cover, but sadly, the majority of people still look down on those who look different. Even many celebrities don't do anything to change this notion of beauty—they become anorexic or bulimic to try to fit that "perfect" mold,

HOW ABOUT YOU?

When **super skinny** celebs like Lindsay Lohan and Nicole Richie say they don't **radically diet** to achieve their slender figures, do you think they're being **honest**?

which teenagers see and then want to copy.

I know how awful it is to feel inadequate. It took my friends to show me that I'm not ugly or worthless. I found support in them when I let them know about my brace and my scoliosis. I learned that I don't need acceptance from other people. I've accepted myself, and I haven't thought any bad thoughts about my body since. In fact, I've learned to love it and couldn't imagine being any different.

Sometimes I still look at people with "perfect" bodies, but then I wonder, *Who really wants that, anyway?* I love my imperfections—they are unique and special in their own way, and I won't let anyone tell me otherwise.

Galit Oren, Age 19

OUTSIDE THE BOX

Do you want to become more comfortable in your own skin? Here are some things to explore in your journal that can help you learn to accept who you are:

- Write down 5 things that you are really good at. This can be anything from skateboarding like a pro to taking care of your cat.
- Disclose one quality that makes you unique.
- If your friends were asked what it is they love about you, what would they say?
- What qualities do you admire in your role models?
- Think about the people who genuinely love you. Do any of them love you because of the way you look?

WHERE DO YOU STAND?

Could you handle it if something
about you stood out from everyone else? How
would you feel if these situations happened to you?

You get the chicken pox and once you're not contagious
anymore, your parents make you go back to school. But you're
still covered with red pockmarks.
- NO BIGGIE   (0 points)
- KINDA BUMMED   (1 point)
- CRISIS MODE   (2 points)

Your little brother has Tourette Syndrome, and a lot of kids
at school just don't understand his condition. They just think
he's weird.
- NO BIGGIE   (0 points)
- KINDA BUMMED   (1 point)
- CRISIS MODE   (2 points)

You're in a serious car accident, and while you escaped major
injury, you are left with a scar along the side of your face.
- NO BIGGIE   (0 points)
- KINDA BUMMED   (1 point)
- CRISIS MODE   (2 points)

You figured you'd be a late bloomer, but never would have
thought that you'd still be the only one in your junior class who
hasn't "developed" yet.
- NO BIGGIE   (0 points)
- KINDA BUMMED   (1 point)
- CRISIS MODE   (2 points)

Your parents lose their jobs and there isn't enough money to
buy new school clothes, so you're stuck wearing your old things,
which are way too small, not to mention seriously out of fashion.
- NO BIGGIE   (0 points)
- KINDA BUMMED   (1 point)
- CRISIS MODE   (2 points)

Add up your points:
   0–3 = You can handle whatever comes along.
   4–7 = Your self-image is a little shaky.
   8–10 = Standing out is your worst nightmare.

I USED TO BUG MY PARENTS TO LET ME WEAR MAKEUP when I was in middle school, but my dad had a "no-makeup rule" until I was sixteen. At the time, I thought his rule was just another example of how my parents liked to torture me, and I longed to be able to wear mascara and eye shadow like everyone else was. I wanted to look and be just like my girlfriends so badly. I just knew that by not wearing makeup and the same designer jeans as everyone else, I was sticking out like a sore thumb.

Seen It?

The famous documentaries by Jean Kilbourne, *Killing Us Softly* (1979) and *Still Killing Us Softly* (1987), were the first to take a critical look at the negative ways in which advertising portrays women.

I had about fifteen minutes before school each morning to brush on the blush and dab on the lip gloss that my friends carried in their purses. I figured that as long as I wiped it off before I got home, what was the difference? But I never stopped to question *why* I wanted to wear makeup so badly. Was it just because everyone else was wearing it? Or was it because I wanted to look older than I was? Or maybe, like this next author questions, I was wearing it to hide what I was feeling inside.

Makeup

Makeup hides my feelings
Makeup hides my face
So many layers of makeup
My true colors can't be traced.

Feelings build up inside me
I'm ready to explode

For Real?

Think about this the next time you want to put on **lipstick**: Most lipsticks contain **fish scales**!

I want someone to talk to
But no one sees my load.

So I wash away the makeup
And show my colors true
I see that someone cares for me
And makes me feel anew.

Ashley Flynn, Age 14

OUTSIDE THE BOX

How many times have you wanted to turn to a friend more than anything, but didn't know how to tell them what it was that you needed? And maybe they desperately wanted to help you through your pain, but they didn't know how to help, or maybe they didn't even know that you needed help in the first place. Here are some ways to let your BFF in on your pain:

- *Be upfront with your friend and let them know what you need. If they're a true friend, they'll want to help, whether it's with a hug, more space or solid advice.*
- *Don't expect your friend to be a mind reader—this will only leave both of you feeling confused and frustrated.*
- *Be appreciative of the things your friends do to help you out, and be there for them when they're the ones in need.*

Take the Quiz:

DO YOU KNOW HOW TO AVOID BEING AN EMOTIONAL BASKET CASE WHEN TOUGH TIMES COME YOUR WAY

1. Things were bad enough in your personal life, and then they got worse when your boyfriend dumped you in a very public way. What's more, he immediately started going out with the biggest snob in school who treats you like dirt. What do you do?

    ___ A. Being dumped by someone you liked so much leaves you feeling worthless and full of self-doubt. You're convinced no one will ever like you "that way" again.

    ___ B. You are shell-shocked by the turn of events and hide out in your bedroom, reminiscing with pictures and notes for a few weeks before finally coming out of your post-breakup fog and getting back on track.

    ___ C. While you didn't see it coming, the fact that your ex so quickly started going out with someone else helps you realize that he's kind of a loser, and losing a loser is actually a good thing!

2. You started out at your new school more than a year ago, but you still haven't managed to make any decent friends. You thought it would be easier to find a place to fit in than it has been. How do you handle it?

    ___ A. You've given it long enough, and clearly you're just not going to ever feel at home at this new school. You decide to withdraw into your own private retreat (your bedroom) and spend any time not at school locked away IMing your old friends.

___ B. You can't help but feel like you don't fit in, but still hold out hope that somewhere at your new school there's a friend waiting in the wings. You don't exert too much effort to find him or her, but don't close off the possibility that they're out there either.

___ C. As hard as it is, you know that the only person who can really make things better for you is *you*. So you decide to sign up for a bunch of clubs and after-school activities and put yourself "out there." You're going to be proactive and find a place to fit in if it's the last thing you do.

3. Your group of friends from elementary school is still hanging out together in middle school, but you've noticed that some of them are changing. You're feeling the pressure to change right along with them, but deep inside you can't help but feel a little bit like a fake. What do you do?

___ A. The thought of dumping your friends and starting over is beyond overwhelming. You go along with the new directions your friends are moving in, figuring it's better to have not-so-great friends than no friends at all.

___ B. You don't like feeling like a fake, but you aren't sure you're ready to do anything about it. You decide to lay low and wait it out—maybe all of your friends are just going through a "phase."

___ C. As much as it scares you to move on and leave your friends behind, you know that doing what your friends are doing just feels wrong for you. Maybe it's time for them to go their way, and you to go yours.

4. Out of nowhere you find you are having trouble dealing with your out-of-control emotions. You've been feeling really down lately, and instead of improving, it seems to be getting worse. How do you deal?

___ A. You know you're spiraling out of control, but you feel helpless to do anything about it. You sink deeper and deeper into your own little world and hope that you'll snap out of your funk soon.

___ B. You aren't ready to ask for help, so instead you try to find healthy ways to release your emotions, like journaling or blogging.

___ C. You know deep down inside that the thoughts going through your head aren't healthy. You find someone you can trust and let them know what's going on.

5. Your best friend of five years suddenly became too cool for words—and definitely too cool to hang out with you anymore. You had always pictured going through high school side by side with her, and now you're feeling a little lost. What do you do?

___ A. You don't accept the changes in your friend, and try to force her to be the person she used to be, confronting her at every turn about the change in her attitude.

___ B. You're bummed out and feel totally confused about what's going on. You write her a letter and explain your feelings, giving her one more chance to make things right with you.

___ C. You are hurt by your friend, but you decide to just let it go and find a new best friend. Clearly you misjudged your friend in the first place, so maybe she's not all that.

Well, how'd you do? Give yourself 10 points for every A, 20 points for every B and 30 points for every C. Look below to find out if you're an emotional basket case waiting to happen:

50–70 points = You struggle with reining in your out-of-control emotions when tough stuff comes along. You need to figure out healthier ways that are personal to you to deal when life doesn't go your way.

80–120 points = You're on an emotional roller coaster, and depending on where you are on the ride, you handle things either really well or really badly. When you handle things well, praise yourself for taking a healthy approach and try to remember to do it the next time something hard comes along.

130–150 points = You have got a serious handle on your emotions, and you know that taking the time to think and sort things out before taking action is always the best bet. Way to go!

CHAPTER 2

HURTING MYSELF

When we're younger, things are just so much simpler, aren't they? Most of us feel good about ourselves, and we haven't become super self-conscious. Relationships with the opposite sex are less complicated because no one has "those" feelings yet. But once we hit puberty and middle school, we get slammed. Suddenly, just about everything feels more complicated, and the reflection in the mirror doesn't always resemble the person we feel like inside. And at a time when we're desperately trying to figure out who we are, for some people the pressure is too much and they start hurting themselves as a way to deal with the confusion they're feeling. This chapter looks at why some teens deal with their feelings of pain in unhealthy ways.

HAVE YOU EVER KEPT A SECRET? I'm not talking about being mum to Mom about who broke her favorite vase or getting a D on a paper. I'm talking big, intense, deep, dark hairy secrets. If you have, you know that keeping a serious secret, especially when it's about something we've done or continue to do that we know isn't right, can be like carrying a huge weight on our shoulders. The pressure can be unbearable, and sometimes the urge to get the secret out in the open is so strong that when it finally does come out (as it almost always does) we can feel our tense muscles breathing a huge sigh of relief.

Read It?

The modern classic novel, *The Best Little Girl in the World*, by Steven Levenkron, is about Kessa, who struggles with a seriously warped body image.

Even though you may sense relief, when secrets this big are finally revealed, things usually don't go back to the way they were. Maybe your friends and family will view you differently. Maybe your routine or your living environment will change. Or maybe something has been put into action that will help you deal with the secret you've been carrying and let you truly move forward.

In this next story, the author's deep, dark secret is finally revealed. And as you'll read, the moment the secret came out was scary and difficult, but without this important first step, things would never get any better.

The Meeting

The office was small and stuffy, with a single window providing an uninspiring view of the cranes and scaffolding that held the promise of a newer, larger high school. The psychologist lounged in his roomy desk chair. The teacher sat at one side of the table, and I perched at the edge of my seat opposite her, muscles clenched to still my trembling. We were an unlikely party—a school psychologist going bald around his ears, a young, serious-faced English teacher and an overachieving sophomore with "everything going for her." But we all had the same problem . . . *me*.

For Real?

The first school psychologist started practicing in 1896, but it wasn't until the mid-1900s that school psychologists became common at most schools.

CONSIDER THIS . . .

Sometimes even parents of teens with **eating disorders** are in **denial** about what's really going on because deep inside they don't want to admit that there's something **seriously wrong** with their child. They're hoping it's just a "phase."

After formal introductions, made difficult by my half-stony, half-petrified silence, my counselor faced me. His smile could have put a saint on guard, and I was feeling far from saintly.

"So, Ashley, I hear from Mrs. O'Connor that you've been having some problems in connection to eating?" he said. Only the presence of my much-loved mentor saved the good doctor from having venom spat in his eye.

I shrugged in response and submitted rather passively to an analysis of why, precisely, I was so obstinate about having my mother find out what close friends and teachers had suspected for months.

"The reason I feel your family should know is that this behavior could be very dangerous to your health," he smoothly replied to my mumble.

CONSIDER THIS . . .

There are **new concerns** that all of the public-health messages about the **rise** in **obesity in kids** will actually result in more teens with eating disorders.

"I'm healthy," I snapped, shifting as my tailbone began to ache from prolonged contact with the chair. "I look fine. If I was so unhealthy, people would have noticed before now."

The psychologist smiled in a satisfied, all-knowing way. "Ah, yes, but you see, a well-known characteristic of eating disorders is that they cause distorted self-image."

I sat very still and tried to block out his words and the images they brought with them, but my mind, so skilled at taking flight in chemistry, remained stubbornly on the topic. Suddenly, the reality of the situation hit me, and the room seemed to grow even smaller. Less than twenty-four hours ago, a secret I had carried alone had slipped out to one person. Now, I was facing the possibility of having my family find out, as if this were truly a real problem. Panic knotted my stomach. I wanted out . . . *now*.

"Please," I said in a low, barely controlled voice. "Miss Kinsley," I said to my teacher, the intensity of the moment causing me to revert to her name from years past. She faced me anxiously.

"Please . . . can we just drop this?" My voice was no more than a whisper, and I felt pressure building behind my eyes with the force of Niagara Falls.

For Real?

An average of 212,000 cubic feet of water flows over Niagara Falls every second. Half of this water pressure is harnessed for power or *hydropower*.

She didn't speak, but I saw the answer in her eyes. They sparkled with tears, and my own began to rain down my cheeks. "I know this is hard, Ashley," she soothed softly. "But we're working with you, not against you. Nothing will be decided today that you're not comfortable with."

Seen It?

The movie *October Sky* (1999) stars Jake Gyllenhaal as a student who has a **supportive teacher** who **encourages** his **dreams** of rocketry.

I stared reproachfully at her sad face, and sobs began to wrack my body, though I tried unsuccessfully to stifle them. I shut my eyes and thought of the life I was missing beyond this small room. I should have been studying for my chemistry test the next period. I had two other tests later in the day. I needed to organize the next meeting of the club for which I served as secretary. I needed to be anywhere but the counseling office. But I was stuck. The secret was out; there was no way to turn back the clock. I had stopped battling the current and was finally hurtling over the waterfall.

The meeting ended shortly thereafter, as my tears hindered me from disclosing any further useful information. The heavy door swung shut as I walked out into the hall. I closed my eyes and tried to take deep breaths to quell the

THE WORD

Hysteria is an emotional outburst, usually resulting from intense fear or panic.

hysteria I felt rising within me.

A hesitant touch on my arm startled me, and I looked up to see Miss Kinsley standing beside me, eyes full of unspoken pain. Wordlessly, she handed me a 3x5 card on which her e-mail address was written, and the words, *Just ask me if you need any help,* were penned with all the precision of an English teacher.

My tears flowed faster as I stared at the card and realized that she had no obligation to me. She had never even been my teacher—only the advisor to my freshman class at homecoming time, and we had grown close throughout the past year and a half.

HOW ABOUT YOU?

Have you ever had a teacher go **above and beyond** for you?

"You don't have to do this," I said.

"But I want to," she said solemnly. "And I mean it. Write to me if you need me over break or the summer."

And I did. I've done it before, and I'll do it again, because in this journey back to health and happiness, I should not have to be alone. And with my teacher by my side—the one who helped me take the most difficult step of my life—I never will be.

Ashley Yang, Age 16

EDITOR'S NOTE: *I recently followed up with Ashley about how this meeting has affected her life. Here's what she had to say: "Since the meeting, outwardly, not many things are different. I still struggle every day with eating, and sometimes it feels nothing has changed. But inwardly, some things have gotten better—I now have a lot of support at school, and the teacher in the story as well as another one are there for me every step of the way, even when I stumble. Even though I feel alone a lot of the time, I know that I'm not and that help is always there.*

Spotlight On... EATING DISORDERS

Look around at the kids in your class, in your church group, at your dinner table. Do you know anyone with an eating disorder? Or maybe you only need look in the mirror to find someone who has a challenging relationship with food.

Eating disorders come in many forms—from the bingeing and purging of bulimia to the starvation of anorexia. Between 5–10 million people in the U.S. have eating disorders, and this number may be grossly underestimated because most people with this psychological illness keep it a secret. And despite what you might think, eating disorders aren't just something that girls deal with. A growing number of boys struggle with body image and eating disorders as well, sometimes leading to dangerous behavior like taking steroids to get the body image they're after.

While it seems logical that eating disorders have to do with food, the truth is, the origins of eating disorders center around psychological and social factors. Here are some of the things that can cause eating disorders:

- Having low self-esteem
- Being the victim of teasing
- Loneliness
- Trouble at home
- Being the victim of abuse
- Being anxious
- Having trouble expressing emotions

For more information, check out the National Eating Disorders Association at *www.nationaleatingdisorders. org*.

Anorexia

You're with me everywhere I go.
You tell me you're my friend.
You slowly kill me every day,
But I try to pretend

That you are here to help me,
You'll bring me friends and fame.
If you gain full control,
A grave will bear my name.

I'm a puppet on a string
And you, the puppeteer.
You control my every move,
You fill my soul with fear.

Each day as you get
    stronger,
You leave no time for
    friends.
You tell me I must exercise—
The torture never ends.

My mind is like a dust storm.
I can't think when you're so
    strong.
And when I try to fight you,
You tell me that I'm wrong.

To think that you will leave me.
You say you'll never go.
I don't need you to live
And I want you to know.

You tell me I'm superior
Because I now am thin.
But what you never told me
Is that what matters lies within.

HOW ABOUT YOU?

Have you ever **felt** like a **negative behavior** or habit has **taken over** your life? How did **you** handle it?

Address Book

If you want to speak to someone about an **eating disorder**, here are some phone numbers where you can find referrals for help:
• Anorexia Nervosa and
  Associated Disorders:
  847-831-3438
  www.ANAD.org
• Rader Programs:
  1-800-841-1515

With help from all my loved ones,
I've learned that it is true.
They love me for the Claire inside,
And so I don't need you.

Anorexia, you're worthless.
And I just want you to know
That I'm ready to recover,
Ready to let you go.

Claire Deden, Age 15

OUTSIDE THE BOX

Do you struggle with a negative body image?
Are you one of thousands of people who see a
distorted reflection in the mirror and are trying to
achieve an "ideal" look? Here are some rational and
positive ways to think about your own body image:

- Be active: A goal of being fit is much
  healthier than a goal of being thin.
- Avoid situations that make you feel bad
  about yourself. If trying on bathing suits in
  a department store always gets you down,
  then don't do it!
- Think about the people you admire. Chances are
  that their physical appearance doesn't have
  anything to do with what makes you like them.
- Write a list of all the things that make you
  special and unique to others, and focus on
  these great qualities instead of feeling down
  about your body.

DO YOU KNOW ANYONE WHO'S STUBBORN?

If I were to name one stubborn person in my family, it would have to be me. I've always tried to view my stubbornness as a good thing. After all, a little stubbornness goes a long way when it comes to being up against a challenge. I'm the one who "keeps on keepin' on," refusing to say "I can't." I'm sure that I can do just about anything by sheer willpower.

But like most things in life, there's a flip side to all of this stubbornness. And the flip side's not so good. Sometimes I'm the last person to ask for help when I really need it, let alone accept help from anyone. In my mind, accepting help would mean that there was something wrong in the first place, or that I was somehow "weak."

I used to think that doing every-thing myself and refusing to accept help would make me look stronger . . . that people would look up to me more, respect me more. But the only thing that happened was that I'd spread myself way too thin and get frustrated. No one thought more of me. If anything, they felt sorry for me.

 **Seen It?**

Maura Tierney's character on *ER*, Abby Lockhart, is one of the most stubborn women in television, and it just about always gets her into trouble.

So, one day while getting ready for a huge after-school project, I accepted help from some friends. Not only did I accept it, I embraced it. I gave people jobs to do, and divided up the respon-sibilities. And you know what? It felt great.

While I'm still a stubborn person, I've definitely been working on the whole "accepting help" thing. Whenever I do, I'm reminded that sometimes letting someone help me when I'm down or in trouble is just what the doctor ordered.

Handing Over My Life

"**T**ry her thigh," an old, husky voice scratched my ringing eardrums like a bug.

"I still can't get anything! This one's drier than a raisin," a younger voice hissed in a panic.

I felt fingers of all different textures on my thigh—the dry, rough calluses of a wood worker; the sweaty, shaky fingers of a little girl; the cool, lotioned fingertips of a princess; the firm, warm fingers of a mother.

Needles pricked here and tourniquets were snapped there as the full cast of fingers fumbled and fought. Finally, the triumphant IV

CONSIDER THIS . . .

Teens today are placing more **pressure** on themselves than ever, including the pressure to **excel at school** and make honor roll. Unfortunately, the pressure can have serious side effects, like an increase in disorders like **anorexia nervosa**.

needle nestled itself into the frightened, ghostly-translucent vein in a smug smirk. I drew the heavy velvet curtains to a close, and empty blankness engulfed my fetal position.

"Anna, do you know where you are? Do you know where you are?" The firm, motherly fingers came into blurry view. She was not a mother, not yet anyhow. In fact, she looked no older than the mere fifteen years that I was. I lifted the heavy metal veils that were my eyelids and squinted.

Alice Bloom, M.D. Her name was prominent against her painfully white scrubs.

M.D.? As in a doctor?

307.1 Anorexia Nervosa. A manila folder poked out from under Dr. Bloom's arm. The shutters dropped over my eyes.

What on earth was I doing in a hospital? Suddenly I was no longer the sweet, timid student known for my 98.9 GPA and perfect attendance record. I was now a disease. Now I was stripped of all my clothing and even branded with a number: *307.1*.

A raspy, hollow whisper cut through the thick, foggy anticipation. "In the hospital," I answered.

"Yes, very good, darling." Dr. Bloom's strawberry-blonde ponytail bobbed enthusiastically.

In a hospital? That's just silly! Hospitals are for sick people—people dying of cancer or AIDS. Not even my honor-roll, analytical mind could wrap itself around why I was dressed in a grotesquely baggy, scratchy hospital gown with a conspiracy of doctors hovering over me like black crows scavenging around a rotten cadaver.

HOW ABOUT YOU?

Have you ever ended up in the **hospital** because you were **sick**? How did **you** handle it?

The mild, delicate aroma of Dr. Bloom's perfume tickled my nostrils. There was a dent on the bed, off to the side of my limp, wired-up figure. The black crows had gone for the night.

My stomach keeled over and flipped as the stench of overly sweet maple syrup snuck past the Plexiglas door frames.

"Wakie, wakie, my dear." A cheery song chirped as the professionally manicured fingernails gently nudged the tray of manila-colored, soggy pancakes in front of my casket. Those hands belonged on an ad for "Nail Perfect" instead of emptying bedpans and bathing the sick.

Fear flooded my over-sized, listless eyes.

Apparently, my fear was written all over my gaunt face. Chin pointed, the sharp contours of my cheeks scrunched together in an odd attempt to scream and cry. But not a sound escaped.

For Real?

Anorexia nervosa needs to be taken seriously. If people with anorexia don't get help, they have a **20%** chance of eventually dying from their disease. **Getting help** from professionals drops those chances to 3%.

The red corners of Nurse Ashley's lips gave in to gravity as she shook her head disapprovingly, as if I were a toddler who spilled her milk for the second time in a row. She reached over to my IV pole, which I had named "Fred," and loaded a fresh bag of "parenteral nutrition."

At long last, my hound ears picked up the shuffling of Dr. Bloom's confident, purposeful, quick shoes. Ignoring the dizziness, I forced my body up into a sitting position.

As soon as the left toe of Dr. Bloom's leather clogs hit the cold, off-white tiles of my room, I ambushed.

CONSIDER THIS . . .

Many doctors and nurses wear **clogs**, in part because they're comfortable, and in part because they promote **good foot health**, especially for people who spend **much of the day on their feet**.

"I want my life back! Do you know that you are making me miss a geometry test right now? Don't I have any say on what happens to my life?!" Overdue angry tears sprang from deep inside my heart.

Dr. Bloom took off her stethoscope and put her arm around my bony back, tenderly supporting me as if I were a porcelain doll going to crack.

Her warm affection went up and down my vertebrae, whispering gently.

"Sometimes you have to give up your life in order to save it. Trust me, you are in good hands."

Jeanne Qiao, Age 15

WHERE DO YOU STAND?

How much do you really know about eating disorders?

1. ☐ ☐   Bulimia is rare in children.

2. ☐ ☐   10% of girls have anorexia nervosa.

3. ☐ ☐   People with eating disorders also often have drug problems.

4. ☐ ☐   Studies show that unrealistic body images portrayed in television shows and magazines don't have any effect on the prevalence of eating disorders.

5. ☐ ☐   Anorexia is a form of a BDD or Body Dysmorphic Disorder.

1. True: Bulimia is actually rare in children and most common in girls in their late teens and early twenties.

2. False: Approximately 1 out of every 100 girls (or 1%) of girls suffers from anorexia nervosa, and 4% of girls are bulimic.

3. True: People with eating disorders often abuse prescription drugs or laxatives in their quest to be thinner.

4. False: Researchers have found a link between an increase in eating disorders in the U.S. and other Western countries and unrealistic body images portrayed in movies, television and magazines.

5. True: Body Dysmorphic Disorder is a newly recognized disease that is defined as being overly concerned with body image. Both boys and girls are plagued with this disease.

NO MATTER HOW STRONG AND SELF-ASSURED WE ARE, with the right kind of pressure and the right timing, many of us can be talked into doing stuff that we normally wouldn't do. I know that for me, that pressure came in the form of someone I've since nicknamed my "bad influence friend." I can remember her waving lit cigarettes in my face saying, "Come on, one cigarette's not gonna kill ya. What are you . . . some kind of straight-laced loser?" (I'm still not sure why I called this girl my friend.)

Fast forward to senior year of college and there I was, smoking cigarettes like it was the coolest thing since sliced bread. All it took was that first little cigarette to get me hooked. (I haven't smoked in years and years by the way . . . I can't even *stand* the smell of smoke!) My point is, I would never have thought in a million years that I would ever smoke cigarettes—I was a runner and an athlete! But smoking, like so many other negative habits, is so addictive— I got hooked without even realizing it. If only I had just said "no" in the first place.

CONSIDER THIS . . .

Addiction doesn't only apply to chemical substances like **alcohol** and **drugs**—behavior can be addictive, too. And just like physical addiction, people who are addicted to behaviors like cutting can have real symptoms of withdrawal such as **severe stress** and **anxiety** if they stop the behavior.

One Cut

"One cut. That's it. That's all," you told me.
"One cut will make you feel stress-free."

"One cut," I said. "That's all it takes.
One cut is such a big mistake."

"One cut," you said, "won't
    hurt. I swear.
One slit on your arm right
    there."

I watched you slit your arm,
    and then I did too.
I don't know why—I guess it
    seemed like the cool thing
    to do.

"One little cut," I told myself.
    "I'll be just fine."
So I started cutting myself all the time.

I became addicted—I needed to cut my arm.
"A few more cuts," I told myself, "won't do any harm."

But then one day, my mom walked in.
"What are you doing? Why'd you start and when?"

These are questions that she said,
As all the memories rushed through my head.

I got help, and now I'm better.
So I wrote you this letter.

When I got home, I asked where
    you were.
"She never got help," Mom said.
    "Something terrible happened
    to her."

For Real?

The average age of a **"cutter"** is 14 years old, and many cutters continue this behavior through their late twenties.

"One cut. That's it. That's all," you said.

And you almost wound up dead.

I know one cut is all it takes.
One cut is such a huge mistake.

Taylor Davis, Age 12

OUTSIDE THE BOX

Are you feeling pressured to try or do something that you're just not into? Here's how to get out of the sitch gracefully:

- Say "no" and mean it. Some people will look for a bit of hesitation and keep pushing. But if you're firm right off the bat, they'll figure they can't change your mind and eventually give up.
- Practice standing up for yourself in a bunch of different situations so it becomes second nature when you're in a really bad spot.
- Try to avoid situations, like parties where there are no adults in sight, where you might be tempted to do something you don't want to do.
- Hang out with friends who'll stand behind you and your decisions, not push you to break them.

HAVE YOU EVER LIED TO YOUR PARENTS? If you're like most teens, your answer is "yes," even if it's only about little things that don't seem like a big deal. I definitely used to lie to my parents, about all kinds of things.

A lot of the times that I lied, I did it in an attempt to avoid getting in trouble. This pretty much never worked—inevitably, my parents always discovered the truth, and when they did, I'd get in a lot more trouble than if I had 'fessed up in the first place. Other times I lied because I didn't want to disappoint them, and I thought the truth wasn't as good as the fiction I could make up.

But the thing I learned about lying is, it's a lose-lose situation. The person you're lying to loses because they don't get the truth, and the liar loses too, because even if they "get away" with the lie, it always stays with them, which can ultimately cause more stress than the truth would have in the first place.

For me, the worst part about lying and then getting caught was knowing that I had let my parents down, and that I'd just further chipped away at the rapidly shrinking wall of trust that I'd started my teen years with. I managed to patch it up from time to time, but I found out that it's a lot harder to build up the trust wall than it is to tear it down.

In this next story, "Class Piggybank," the author gets caught up in a lie that takes over her life until she finds a way to wipe the slate clean.

Class Piggy Bank

Someone once said to me, "Why do you read so much? Is it because you hate everyone and don't want to be around us?" I didn't answer her question, but I knew why I buried myself in books: It was because I didn't want to give anyone

For Real?

75% of **teens** report that they **read** for pleasure on most days, and they rate it as more important than math and writing when it comes to things they need to learn if they want to be **successful**.

a chance to ever hurt me again.

My reputation was set in stone in my new middle school by the only kid I knew, Juliette, and it made my first year a nightmare. Juliette was horrid to me—she made up lies about me and twisted everything I said. In no time, she had managed to turn the whole class against me.

So I gave up on my classmates and put my energy somewhere else—I decided to read. No one could get on my case about reading. Reading was "normal." So I read at recess, lunchtime, in the Metro and in study hall. I was always stuck inside a book and wouldn't come out until after the bell rang. I read and read and read. *Harry Potter, Princess Diaries, Redwall* and on and on. I never got tired of reading. When I would stop reading, my classmates threw insults my way, so I jumped back into a book to escape from the real world.

But I was lonely, and even though books gave me some happiness, I was alone. So I decided to change, to become another person. I started wearing more stylish clothes, wanting to look the same as everyone else.

Read It?

A Northern Light by Jennifer Donnelly features 16-year-old Mattie, whose love of books and words inspires her dream of being a writer.

By seventh grade, I finally had made two friends. I felt happy and so blessed to have them. But unfortunately, it was not to last. Just before Christmas, my new friends said that I was "out" and

Juliette was "in." Juliette looked so happy about my situation, and she'd rub it in. "No more friends for you. You *lost!*" she'd say.

THE WORD

A **euro** is the currency in Europe, just like the dollar is the currency in the U.S.

I was devastated. Not only was my heart ripped in two, but people made fun of me, especially about the fact that I was alone. I didn't defend myself. Instead, I took it out on my mom.

My mom was an angel, while I was a brat, always crying, screaming about my class. My mom listened patiently and tried to help, encouraging me to be true to myself. She was always trying to make me laugh.

CONSIDER THIS . . .

Do you ever **feel** like your parents just **don't listen** to you? Well, they might say the same thing about you. In fact, the number-one issue for most parents is that their teenagers don't communicate with them enough.

She didn't deserve what I did next.

I started stealing from her. At first it was only a euro or two, but still I was stealing—stealing from the only one who was always behind me. I felt like I needed the money to buy key rings or books, even chocolate baguettes, just to make me happy. I bought magazines to fill the empty pages in my planner like my classmates had done.

Within a couple of days, my popular classmates started asking me for money. I thought, *Why not?* I knew I was being a pushover, but I didn't dare speak up because I didn't want to be even more of a reject than I already was. So I became my class's piggy bank. And I had to steal a lot more than before if I wanted to keep it up.

For Real?

More than $16 billion dollars worth of merchandise is **stolen** each year in the U.S. Nearly **50%** of shoplifters are teens.

Soon, twenty or fifty euros were finding their way into my pockets every day. I was scared because I knew I was doing something against the law. I was so afraid that I jumped out of my skin whenever the telephone rang. Like old yogurt, I was going bad. I felt guilty all the time. I wanted to stop, but every time I saw my mom's wallet, I wanted the money too badly.

Eventually, my mother discovered that her wallet was being emptied. She and my father asked me many times if I was stealing, but every time, I lied and said "no." I felt really bad about lying, but I was relieved that it worked. And even though my father was convinced I was lying, they gave me the benefit of the doubt.

One day, the strain was too much. After I went to a candy shop, my mom questioned me about my outing. I was so nervous, I found myself unfolding the whole story. I remembered every single detail. My parents listened and didn't interrupt, which was good because once I started, it was hard to stop.

I was so ashamed of myself, and I could see that my parents were very disappointed. It ripped my heart in two. If I used to be mad about my actions, now I was appalled. I tried in vain to keep my breath even, but I could feel the

HOW ABOUT YOU?

Many of us would **rather** get **yelled** at by our parents than have them give us the silent, **"disappointed"** treatment. How about you?

tears rolling down my cheeks. I heard my parents speaking but it didn't reassure me at all. If only they would yell at me, then I wouldn't have felt so awkward. There was almost absolute silence, except for the sound of my pounding heart.

In the end, my parents forgave me. My punishment was that my mom would keep a record of my money until after Christmas and cut my allowance in half. Today, my mom and I are fine. It took a while before she trusted me again, but now she trusts me completely. I was thrilled that everything went back to normal, but I will never forget the feelings of stealing, never being able to trust anyone, always afraid of being found out.

Surprisingly, Juliette is the one having problems with her friends now. I actually feel sad for her and want to stand up for her, even after everything she did. I wouldn't want anyone to have to go through what I went through, not even Juliette.

CONSIDER THIS . . .

The **family dinner table** isn't just a place to grab some grub. Teens who sit down and have dinner with their family on a regular basis are **less likely** to try **drugs, drink** or **smoke**.

As for me, I'm more careful how I treat my mom. I know how it feels to be hurt, so I do my best to be a better daughter. When I mess up, I apologize as quickly as I can, and I'm happy to say that today, our relationship is better than ever. I guess you could say that in some way, I'm glad I went through this whole experience, because things are better now than they've ever been. And while sometimes I wish I could have learned what I did in a different way, maybe I had to go through what I did to get here.

Lucille Taquet, Age 13

OUTSIDE THE BOX

If you've ever broken the trust between you and your parents, you know that it can be hard to get back to where you were. Here are some tips for regaining the trust:

- Be patient: It takes a lot longer to build up the trust than it did to break it. It might take a while for parents, and the only way to get what you want is to give them time to come around.
- Be consistent: A long track record of situations where you acted trustworthy will go a long way.
- Be ready to do whatever it takes to get your parents' trust back.
- Be genuine and accept the consequences of your actions. Your parents need to feel that you truly "get it."

THIS NEXT STORY, "STAY CURIOUS," is such a powerful and personal look at one teen's struggle with mental illness that we felt it was important to include in this book. As the author came to grips with the confusion and frustration he was experiencing over a need to figure out the meaning of life, he realized that sometimes the *mystery* of life, and the challenges we face along the way, are what living is really about.

Stay Curious

"**S**tay curious."

That's what a man named Bill Phillips said after winning the Nobel Prize for physics back in 1997. What an interesting man he

was—he knew more mysteries of the universe than I will ever hope to. I met him only a few months ago, but that's not what this story is about . . . not really, anyway.

It all started on a brisk November day. I woke up more ticked off than Hulk Hogan. I put on my headphones, blasting Nirvana's "Oh Me," and headed off to the School of the Arts in upper North Charleston, South Carolina. I was a creative writing major, and a good one at that. I had no idea that in a few months' time, I would win a National Scholastic Art and Writing Award for a humorous short story I had written, or that I would be published in a book of poems. But what happened between those triumphs and that bleak November day was much more important.

I stepped onto the bus, Kurt Cobain still yelling in my ears, and glared at all the expectant, judgmental minds before me.

Read It?

Come As You Are: The Story of Nirvana by Michael Azerrad is a rock biography of the band that was written before lead singer Kurt Cobain's death in 1994.

Finding a seat on this bus was like catching a tadpole in the English Channel, but I was good at it, and I always loved a challenge. I spotted a seat in the middle of the bus and sprang for it.

I felt angry. I hated everyone around me—the kids on the bus, the people driving by . . . everyone. The oddest part was that I hated them all for no apparent reason. I remember cursing them all under every breath, even my family. I knew I loved them dearly, but I just couldn't stop feeling hatred.

Seen It?

The Academy Award-winning film *A Beautiful Mind* (2001) stars Russell Crowe as mathematician John Nash, who, despite his schizophrenia, went on to win the Nobel Prize.

That day I came home from school and told my parents how mad I was. They asked me why and didn't understand when I said simply: "I have no idea." It scared them, and it scared me. But I didn't have time to be scared—I was busy thinking all the time. And I mean *all the time.* I didn't sleep. I hardly ate. I didn't do homework. I disregarded my teachers. I did nothing but *think,* because that's what Nobel Prize-winner Bill Phillips told me to do. I pondered the universe, mathematics, physics, chemistry. I thought about it all—space, time, light, energy, motion, matter, mass, the whole deal. I wanted to know everything, and I wanted to know it *now.* I knew I could change the world with my brain, that I could show these scientists things they never imagined. The only thing I didn't know was that I was wrong.

I ended up in the Institute of Psychiatry nearby. I had a four-day stay because I couldn't get my mind

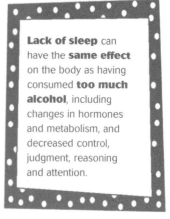

Consider This . . .

Lack of sleep can have the **same effect** on the body as having consumed **too much alcohol**, including changes in hormones and metabolism, and decreased control, judgment, reasoning and attention.

to shut off. Because of the lack of sleep, I hallucinated greatly. I heard my name being called when I was alone. I saw animals that jumped out of thin air, and my greatest delusion of all was that I thought I was doing the right thing. At the hospital, they tried to tell me that if I ever wanted to be a real physicist and study our world, I had to do homework and try hard in school.

"Screw that!" I said. "I'll make it without you all! I have a mind like you won't even believe! I don't need you." I wished so hard that this was all true, but I had known the whole time I was wrong.

So after I was discharged from the "loony bin," as my friends called it, I did half-decent in school. I did a good bit of my homework, I wrote like crazy for my class, and I didn't think much about anything. Then the confusion gates flung open once more, and this time they were really wide. I

THE WORD

The word **loony** comes from the word "lunatic," which originally referred to an old belief that people acted odd depending on what phase the moon (or *luna*) was in.

had started thinking again, wondering things like, *Why are we here? What am I supposed to do? Is school really important? What happens when I die?* Most people stop asking these questions at age six or seven, but once more, I wanted the answers—and I wanted them now. So I bought textbooks and magazines and looked on the Internet to find every scrap of innovative science I could get my hands on. But I got zilch, nothing, *nada.* And just when I was going to give up, my hallucinations kicked back in.

I remember the night perfectly. I was in my room crying because I couldn't find the answers I was looking for anywhere.

I had four light bulbs hanging from the fan on my ceiling, and they were casting shadows on my wall. I stopped my sobbing and looked at them for a moment. I remember thinking, *Wow, that's beautiful.* Then they started to move and rearrange. I saw two giant eyes and then a mouth of shadow. I gaped in amazement, and then the face started to open and close its mouth in laughter, laughing at me. I was a loser, I had ruined my eighth-grade GPA in neglect, and I had upset my entire family who was sick of me yelling at them for tiny things. I had lost all my friends because I called them all individually and told them exactly why I hated them. I had nothing, which was why this monster of light and shadow was laughing at me—he knew I had hit rock bottom.

"Shut up! Shut up!" I screamed. I ran to my parents' room and woke them up screaming. I told them everything, from my quest for the answers to the reason I didn't sleep. The next morning, they brought me back to the hospital.

I was on the inpatient floor for four days again before they brought me up to the fifth floor, where I would spend the next three months of my life, bringing it all back in order. I had to force into my head that education was the only way I would make it, and that everyone has great things to offer the world. I had to learn to see the good in anything, rather than the worst in everything. I cried and I screamed, and sometimes even spoke civilized to the staff on the fifth floor, who were kind enough to listen. They played poker with me and my fellow patients, and they drew our blood for tests. They told us when to eat and sleep, and we were grateful for it. That kind of control was the greatest blessing I will ever have, other than the love of my family. I didn't have to worry about my next meal—

WHERE DO YOU STAND?

Do you know how to get help when you need it?
Would you do any of the following?

___ YES ___ NO When you look in the mirror, you don't like what you see, and it's forcing you to engage in some drastic and unhealthy eating behavior. Do you call a hotline for eating disorders and get some advice?

___ YES ___ NO You've been having some pretty bad thoughts lately and you know that the way you're feeling just isn't right, or safe. You're afraid you might hurt yourself. Would you confide in a trusted teacher or parent about what's going on in your head?

___ YES ___ NO Someone you love has a problem with alcohol, and their behavior is having a serious impact on you. You've done your best to try and curb their drinking, but you realize that you can't fix their problem. Would you seek out the help of a support group like Alateen?

___ YES ___ NO You thought that making yourself throw up was something you would try and then never do again, but before you know it, you're completely addicted to bingeing and purging. Would you realize that you need professional help and talk to someone who can point you in the right direction?

___ YES ___ NO You see some friends from school playing the "pass-out game" at a party. You know that this game is actually deadly. Do you call someone to come to the party and break things up?

If you answered "yes" to at least two of these questions, then you've got a good attitude about knowing when and how to ask for help. If you answered "yes" to fewer than two, don't forget that asking for help isn't a sign of weakness, but one of strength.

they gave it to me. I didn't have to worry about my school work—I got it in portions through the mail. I didn't have to worry about keeping the thoughts in my head—I could talk about them openly to a room full of people. I was in paradise.

My hallucinations stopped, and I sewed each section of my childhood back together carefully, to make sure I would get a second chance. I went back into school and tried my best to make up the work. I read my science journals in portions and knew exactly when to stop. The men and women in that hospital were my undeserving gift from God, my crutches to walk on until seen fit by others. I thank them every night before I sleep, though they can't hear me. It's because of them that I can sleep at all.

The following summer I took part in a program at Clemson University where I spent two weeks with a physics professor, taking physics and calculus. It was the most fun I'd ever had—we were solving problems of the cosmos together! He even told me I was one of the three mathematical geniuses he had ever met, but I was the only crazy one. I am a freshman in high school now, and I am still at the School of the Arts, writing every day. My GPA is somewhere in the high 3s, and I plan to apply to a science and mathematics school when I'm a junior. It's been quite a ride these last two years, and one constant got me through it all, and that's this: the trick to keeping a healthy lifestyle is not trying to stay in the known parts of life, because things you don't expect are what makes it all interesting. Instead, try to live in the unknown. It's the only way to *stay curious*.

Ian Brown, Age 15

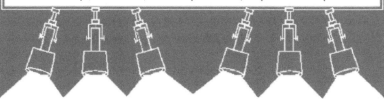

Spotlight On . . .
MENTALL ILLNESS IN TEENS

So what is mental illness, anyway? Mental disorders are considered biological conditions of the brain—they have nothing to do with intelligence, and they can't be controlled by willpower. Different kinds of mental illness include things like obsessive-compulsive disorder, schizophrenia, depression, ADD and ADHD, and bipolar disorder.

Between 5% and 9% of children 5- to 17-years-old have some form of mental illness. And while that might seem like a scary statistic, the truth is, between 70% and 90% of people with mental disorders can have a major reduction of their symptoms with the right treatment. In fact, millions of people with mental illness live very fruitful lives. Some are even at the top of their game, like Carrie Fisher (actress), Jane Pauley (newscaster), Terry Bradshaw (former NFL player) and Tipper Gore (wife of former Vice President Al Gore).

Here are some of the signs that people with untreated mental illness might have:

- Serious depression
- Intense physical anxiety about everyday things
- Eating disorders
- Overly angry and aggressive behavior
- Delusions and bizarre ideas
- Being overly withdrawn and unable to handle social situations
- Suicidal thoughts

For more info and resources on mental illness, check out: *www.mentalhelp.net.*

Take the Quiz:
ARE YOU COMFORTABLE IN YOUR OWN SKIN ❓

1. You've always been the skinny one in your family, and you ate whatever you wanted without a second thought. But as your body starts going through the changes of puberty, you've noticed that your limbs, which used to look like sticks, are now plumped up from muscle and fat. Your family has been teasing you about the changes. How do you feel?

   ___ A. You are extremely sensitive, and your family's teasing is the last straw. You put aside your favorite pair of pre-body-change jeans and make a secret pact with yourself to fit inside them by the end of summer vacation.

   ___ B. Even though you don't think you look fat, you still find yourself kind of surprised (and not so pleased) at your new profile every time you catch a glimpse of yourself in the mirror.

   ___ C. You embrace your new figure, curves and all. You know that it's just part of growing up—and who wants to look like a kid forever?

2. One of your legs is shorter than the other . . . always has been, always will be. Up to now this has been no biggie—you just wear a special shoe on the shorter leg to make things even. But you find that the kids at your new middle school aren't so accepting of you and your special shoes, and the stares are starting to get to you. How do you handle it?

   ___ A. You can't help but feel more self-conscious about your special shoes and try to overcompensate for your differences by proving to the kids at your new school that you're really cool and worth knowing.

   ___ B. You know that the only way people can get to you is if you let them. You've dealt with your physical challenge your whole life, and you decide not to give your power away by letting others make you feel self-conscious.

___ C. You start wearing longer flare-bottomed pants to hide your shoes and become very secretive every time you have to change in the locker room for gym class. You begin to resent the fact that you're different from everyone else.

3. You've always been somewhat scrawny, and this has been no big deal up until now, when suddenly the other guys in the locker room all seem to have muscles that rival a bodybuilder. Suddenly your lack of muscles is something you can't ignore any longer. How do you feel?

___ A. You take a look at your dad and brother and realize that genetically speaking, muscle bound you are not. You don't sweat it . . . who wants to be known as a muscle head anyway?

___ B. While not being muscular wasn't a big deal before, now that you're crushing on a pretty girl in school, you feel like without muscles, you have no chance. You notice some guys in school are taking steroids to change their body and decide to get in on the action.

___ C. You wish you could build more muscle and decide to spend extra hours at the gym each week pumping iron. Even if you can't look like Mr. America, why not try to have the best body you can have?

4. You see a new movie starring way-too-thin actresses, and spend most of the movie focused on how skinny they are instead of how thin the plot is. When the movie is over, you go to the restroom and take a good, hard look at yourself. What do you see?

___ A. You step back and spin around, trying to see what your butt looks like in your jeans and are devastated to realize it looks nothing like the girls on the big screen. You leave feeling inadequate and down about yourself.

___ B. You were feeling confident before the movie, but now, looking at your reflection, you can't help but feel a little less attractive. It takes you a few days to bounce back and feel confident in who you are again.

___ C. You see the same girl you saw before you went into the theater. Your body is your body, and you love it for what it is. Those girls might starve themselves to achieve their impossible figures, but you know you could never be a good athlete and look like them.

5. You're fifteen years old, and while you've shot up in height, your body hasn't made any of the other changes that all of your friends have gone through, especially when it comes to the breast department. How do you handle it?

___ A. You begin to fantasize about having perfect perky breasts like so many girls on TV, and you research breast-enhancement surgery. You know that until you have a big chest, you'll never feel good about yourself.

___ B. You realize that all women are built differently, and you'll be cool with however your body turns out. You admire the women in Hollywood who buck the trend of breast-enhancement surgery, like Kirsten Dunst.

___ C. You try to disguise your flat-chestedness by wearing padded bras and keep your fingers crossed that your body will kick into action soon.

So, are you comfortable in your own skin? Give yourself the following points:

1. a = 30, b = 20, c = 10; 2. a = 20, b = 10, c = 30; 3. a = 10, b = 30, c = 20; 4. a = 30, b = 20, c = 10; 5. a = 30, b = 10, c = 20.

50–70 points = You couldn't be more comfortable with who you are. You've always had a strong self-image and know that how you feel about yourself is the most important factor in how successful you are in life. You are who you are with confidence and pride.

80–120 points = You've got good days and bad days when it comes to your self-image, and the littlest thing can change how you feel about yourself on any given day. When you're having a bad day, do something that makes you feel good about yourself, like playing a sport you're good at, to remind yourself that your body is capable of doing a lot of amazing things.

130–150 points = You're so displeased with the body you've been given that sometimes you wish you could find a new skin to be comfortable in. Try focusing on things in life that are less superficial than looks and fashion, and celebrate the things about you that are uniquely you.

CHAPTER 3

FAMILY AFFAIRS

No matter what our family situation—parents together, parents divorced, only child or more siblings than you care to mention—they all come with their own baggage, and they all have an effect on who we are and how we view the world. This next chapter looks at different challenges that some teens face when it comes to their family life.

IT SEEMS LIKE THERE'S SO MUCH TALK ABOUT MARRIAGES in the news these days—debates over who can and can't get married, high-profile relationships like Jen and Brad or Jessica and Nick falling apart in a very public way. Flip open a newspaper or magazine and chances are you'll find a story about a great marriage or a disastrous one. And the reality is, the statistics are pretty grim. Fifty-seven percent of marriages today will end in divorce. Are your parents part of this majority? Or is the very idea of your parents splitting up completely foreign to you?

My parents are one of the minority . . . they're still together after more than forty years, so I don't have any firsthand experience about what it's like to go through such a painful split. But I've watched enough friends go through their parents' divorce, and now have witnessed friends themselves getting divorced, and I've realized that no matter what the circumstances, no matter how friendly (or vicious) the whole procedure is, divorce resembles a natural disaster as devastating as any hurricane or earthquake. Destruction, sadness and confusion over how to start over lie in its wake.

In Between

Being kidnapped was nothing like it's made to seem on television. There were no creepy men in vans offering lollipops or dramatically filmed police chases. In fact, for me, being kidnapped simply meant missing a flight from New Orleans to Seattle.

I had been in New Orleans visiting my mom during my fifth-grade winter vacation, and she had decided that I was

Read It?

In Joy Nicholson's book *The Tribes of Palos Verdes* (1998), Medina Mason tries to cope with her parents' disintegrating marriage by turning to surfing.

not going to be returning to my dad's. To this day I still don't remember the decisive moment when my parents separated. For as far back as I can recall, I've been part of two distinct families, often located thousands of miles apart. Because of this I have been able to avoid the "If only things were like they were before" lamenting that many children of broken families fall into. The fact that my parents were divorced has never been the paramount issue. What has caused so much pain over the years has been the vehement custody battles and my role as messenger for two very confused and upset adults. When I think about the effects of being turned into a commodity by my parents, I

For Real?

More than a quarter of **kids** in the United States live in **single-parent homes**.

think of cancer. I see them in different areas of my life: I have little belief in the sanctity of marriage, and as of yet have minimal desire to bring my own children into the world. In relationships, I rarely feel comfortable completely revealing my soul. Years of therapy have proved helpful, but honestly, no cure looms on the horizon, and I remain in a constant struggle to live in mental health.

Consider This . . .

The historic city of **New Orleans** was forever changed when Hurricane Katrina came ashore on August 29, 2005, bringing with it a wall of water called a **storm surge**. Later, levees were breached, and water flooded the city.

Through much of my childhood, I lived in a fog of confusion— confused as to why my parents had separated in the first place, confused about why they seemed angry every time they spoke to each other, and confused about why, if they both really did "want the best for me" (their shared mantra), they had such different notions of what "best" meant.

Best for my dad meant, among other things, living with him. And for a while, my mom agreed. She had been attending medical school in New Orleans, and her packed schedule and menial income made raising a child nearly impossible.

When I flew from Seattle to New Orleans back in fifth grade, I was elated to be leaving behind the cold and the wet for the sunshine of the Big Easy. The trip seemed perfectly ordinary with requisite visits to the zoo, the children's museum and my favorite restaurant, Kim Sum, the best Vietnamese food in New Orleans. Then one day my mom informed me that we would be visiting a local elementary school in the afternoon, "just to see if you like it." I didn't really see

HOW ABOUT YOU?

Do you share time between **two households** and **two parents**? How do you deal?

For Real?

In 1970, author James Conaway published a crime novel set in New Orleans called *The Big Easy*, which helped make the nickname for the city stick.

For Real?

More than 11 million **marriages end** in **divorce** every year.

a reason to be visiting schools, but I went along with it.

That afternoon I visited Isidore Newman School. I disliked the idea of wearing uniforms, but coming from a public school I was impressed by the number of computers and a science curriculum that involved experiments using more ingredients than those found in most household kitchens. The next day we visited another school, the prestigious Metairie Park Country Day School. With a sprawling and stately campus as well as an absence of uniforms, Country Day was immediately to my liking. Yet, even as we visited schools, it never occurred to me that I would be attending them any time soon, especially not at the end of my winter vacation. I had just moved to Seattle from San Francisco the previous summer, and I was still adjusting to *that* move. When I went one afternoon to do IQ testing, it still didn't click in my head what my mom was planning.

The day before I was supposed to return to Seattle, she finally told me what was going on. She talked about my future and how hard it was for her never to see me before she dropped the bomb.

"Tally," she said, "you're not going back to Seattle tomorrow.

CONSIDER THIS . . .

People are split in the U.S. on how they feel about **private versus public schools**. Opponents of private school say that they're elitist and just fuel more classism because of the high tuition, while proponents say that if they can afford to pay for smaller classes and more prestige, then why not?

For Real?

IQ tests were first used in the early 1900s in France, where they helped separate out children with learning disabilities from "normal" children.

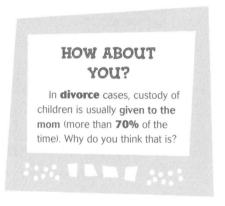

HOW ABOUT YOU?

In **divorce** cases, custody of children is usually **given to the mom** (more than **70%** of the time). Why do you think that is?

You're going to stay here and live with me."

What? My mind was racing. *Stay here? In the city where I fall asleep to the sound of gunshots, fearful of the shadows on my wall? Here in the city where I can't walk down the street to the corner store by myself? Here? A city that is definitely not my home?*

There were tears and wailing and screaming, followed by my mother's arguments that did nothing to assuage my grief. After myriad swells and calms in the storm, I finally found myself on the phone with my father. One can only imagine his confusion and anger, but he managed to speak to me calmly, promising, "Everything will be all right."

The next few days were a blur of emotions. I continued talking to my dad on the phone, but each time my mom would also be on the line. Maybe she feared he would give me instructions to run away or call the police—I've yet to ask her about it. Midway through the week, I began school at Metairie Park Country Day. Having moved around a lot when I was younger allowed me to quickly feel comfortable in new situations. Country Day was no different. By the end of the week, I'd come to accept that I'd be living in New Orleans for the rest of the year. I did my homework, made friends and adjusted to my new life while trying not to dwell on the fact that I really wasn't supposed to be there. Every time I talked to my dad, he still insisted that I would be coming home soon, and neither of my parents took the time to explain what was going on or why they had such divergent views about where I should be living. A stuffed snow tiger named Stripes served as my confidante, his plush easily wicking away my tears.

Explaining my situation to my new classmates and teachers was too daunting, as I barely understood it myself. I informed people simply that I had moved to New Orleans and hoped they wouldn't ask too many follow-up questions.

For Real?

The **first submarine attack** in world history happened during the American Revolution in **1776** when a small submarine called the Turtle attempted (*and failed at*) a surprise attack in New York Harbor.

Less than a week later, I heard a loud rapping on the front door of our apartment. I looked up midway through a sentence about the American Revolution to see two police officers and a man I'd never seen before at the door. I ran upstairs to my room, but was quickly called back down. I grabbed Stripes as I made my way downstairs. The scene that confronted me was surreal: three police officers, two men in trench coats (who I later found out were lawyers), and both my mother and father sobbing. While I was obviously the prize of this looting squad, no explanation was given to me beyond that I was going back to Seattle.

I was furious. Having finally adjusted to my new home, I was once again being uprooted against my will. I sat crying in the back of one of the lawyer's sedans. I refused to acknowledge anyone, choosing to remain mute—it was the

Seen It?

Perhaps one of the most famous classic films about a custody battle is the Academy Award–winning *Kramer vs. Kramer* (1984) starring Dustin Hoffman and Meryl Streep.

only control that I had over the situation, and I desperately needed control when everything was in such a state of flux. I hoped to remain silent forever, but after three days I accidentally spewed out a "thank you" to a waitress refilling my water glass.

Today, my whole family lives in Seattle, and I divide my time equally between two households. I still find it amazing how selfishly parents can act when it comes to "wanting the best" for their children. The animosity I felt toward my mother and father for their actions has slowly melted away to reveal a previously unknown capacity for forgiveness. As I have matured, I've tried to shed myself of much of the baggage willed to me by my parents. I've begun to take responsibility for and solve my problems instead of simply blaming them on my parents. Freeing myself from this weight has been a tremendously uplifting experience. The resolve I've gained from past tribulations continues to prove valuable in confronting the world each day. Life truly is a beautiful struggle.

Tally Bower, Age 17

OUTSIDE THE BOX

Starting a new school? Here are some survival tips to get you through the first week:

- Get enough sleep and eat breakfast so you feel on top of your game.
- Keep notes of important info, like your locker combination and schedule, handy so you can feel confident about what you're doing and where you're going.
- Wear clothes that you feel good and comfortable in.
- Try sitting in different desks in your classes each day to increase your chances of meeting someone.
- Find out where important rooms are—the bathroom, the caf, etc.—right off the bat.

Spotlight On... DIVORCE

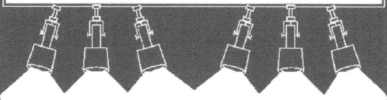

More than half of today's marriages end in divorce, so it's no surprise that there is a whole generation of teens today who come from "broken families." But no matter how common divorce is, it doesn't get any easier to handle, especially for kids caught in the middle.

If you or a friend are dealing with a family breaking up, here are some ideas for keeping a grip:

• Try not to get in the middle of the fighting. This might be easier said than done, especially if you feel one of your parents is more responsible for the divorce than the other.

• Don't blame yourself for what's going on. Many teens can't help but feel as if they're responsible for the breakup of the marriage, even if only in a small way. But the reality is, it's not about you . . . it's about them. In fact, right about now, you and your happiness are most likely the biggest things on your parents' minds.

• Know that sometimes parents who are divorced can actually be happier than those who remain unhappily married.

• Talk to someone about what's going on. Now is definitely the time to lean on friends, family, siblings, mentors. Use whatever resources you have for emotional support—don't be shy!

A great Web site for support and resources when it comes to divorce can be found at the KidsHealth Web site: *www.kidshealth.org/teen/your_mind/families/divorce.html.*

I CAUGHT AN EPISODE OF *OPRAH* the other day, and I saw a true story that brought me to tears. A mom had been diagnosed with cancer and was facing a death sentence. Since her daughter was only five years old at the time, she recorded hundreds of hours of video messages to her daughter so she'd have a chance to share all of the stories and advice that she would have done were she there for her daughter's teen years.

If that wasn't sad enough (picture me sitting on my couch sobbing by this point), one of the mom's messages to her daughter was about the fact that she wanted her husband to eventually remarry after she passed away and that the daughter should accept the new mom into her life with open arms. And there sitting on Oprah's couch was the young girl, now thirteen years old, embracing her dad's new wife, whom she is proud to call "Mom."

While this story is bittersweet, having a parent remarry after the death of a spouse can bring up some pretty intense and confusing emotions, as the author of this next poem, "The Way Things Used to Be," expresses so honestly.

CONSIDER THIS . . .

Making **children** a significant part of a **marriage** ceremony after one of the spouses has died is one way to make the transition **easier**.

The Way Things Used to Be

I took for granted the times we had,
The moments we laughed until we cried.
Those late-night talks,
The simple words that turned a bad day into good.
It used to be just you and me.
What was wrong with the way it used to be?

After Dad died, you said that you
    could never fall in love again.
You were wrong.

As I sit here, watching you walk
    down the aisle,
I can't help but wonder—
Is Dad watching? Does he approve?
I know he wants you to be happy,
But do you really need a man to make you happy?

I've never had to share you.
Call me selfish, but I liked it that way.
You say Dad can never be replaced.
Now you're saying your vows that are
    supposed to last forever—
"Until death do us part."

If death parts you, does that mean
    you have to find someone new?
I don't want Dad to be replaced.

Even though you say he never will
    be, it sure feels like it.
It feels like you're marrying into
    something that is taking Dad's place.
I don't want him to take on the
    fatherly role.

I want things to be the way they
    used to be.

Neda Bewren, Age 17

For Real?

When a **spouse dies**,
the surviving spouse can be
plagued with declining health
and financial problems, which
is one reason why widows
and widowers remarry.

Seen It?

In the tearjerker
Stepmom (1998),
Julia Roberts stars
as a woman who marries
a man whose ex-wife is
losing her battle with
cancer.

CONSIDER THIS . . .

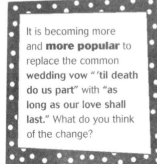

It is becoming more
and **more popular** to
replace the common
**wedding vow "'til death
do us part"** with **"as
long as our love shall
last."** What do you think
of the change?

WHERE DO YOU STAND?

How much do you really know about these family circles?

1. T F Just like humans, most primates form monogamous, "nuclear" families with a man, woman and children.

2. T F Since as dolphins are mammals, their family structure is exactly like human families in every way, as their children stick close to their parents for more than 15 years.

3. T F Even though the female penguin lays the eggs, the male penguin spends the same amount of time nesting the eggs as his mate does.

4. T F The Disney movie *The Lion King* realistically showed the family structure of a lion family, or pride.

5. T F When a baby elephant is upset, the whole family comes over and comforts him or her.

1. False: While a few primates, like gibbons and siamangs, form monogamous families, most primates hang together in large social groups, and the males and females have multiple relationships.

2. False: Young dolphins stay with their mothers for anywhere between 3 and 6 years before going their own way.

3. True: Right after the female penguin lays one to two eggs, she leaves them behind with her mate so she can go out for a few weeks in search of food. When she comes back, it's her turn to nest, while the male goes out for food.

4. False: Lion "prides" are made up of up to 20 females and their cubs, as well as 2 to 3 males who are in charge. In *The Lion King*, Simba's father and then Simba himself was the only head lion in charge.

5. True: Elephants are sensitive creatures indeed! If the baby in the family cries or acts upset, the rest of the family will come over to stroke it with their trunks as a form of comfort.

WHEN I WAS A KID, cable television, let alone pay channels like HBO and Showtime, were something only a few lucky kids had. (My parents *still* don't have cable television, so you can guess how they felt about all of the racy content on MTV and other cable channels when I was in high school.) So for us, the highlight of our at-home entertainment came in the form of the CBS Sunday Night Movie and the like, which usually starred some "B" or "C" actor and featured some overly dramatic scenario, like the Earth is about to implode because someone was drilling too deep into its core or a bizarre experiment creates super mosquitos capable of spreading disease faster than a speeding bullet.

HOW ABOUT YOU?

Do you feel like **everything** happens for a **reason**, or do you think events in your life are more **random**?

Many of these made-for-TV movies were so over the top that they were beyond unbelievable (which is probably why they were on television instead of on the big screen). The stakes were high, and the cheesy acting factor even higher.

But what happens when real life starts to resemble a made-for-TV movie? What happens when the wildest scenario is suddenly taking place behind the four walls of your house? Like the author of this next story discusses, sometimes letting go—of expectations, of false hopes, of anger—is the only way to deal.

Letting Go

Back when I was in the fourth grade, my family was picture perfect. If you can imagine a "Beaver Cleaver"-type family that was always going to church and looked like the ideal, well, that was us. But things aren't always what they seem. It took me a while to figure that out, but I did. And it was a lesson I learned the hard way.

Seen It?

The saying "Beaver Cleaver" comes from the 1950s sitcom, *Leave It to Beaver*, which starred the "all-American family," the Cleavers. Beaver was the youngest son.

My dad got a new job that was about an hour's drive away, so he was only home on the weekends. I didn't really think that much of it at the time until I noticed that Mom started to seem constantly upset. It just wasn't like her.

I remember what happened next like it was yesterday. My dad sat the family down and told us that he had something important to talk with us about. Then came the worst news: Mom and Dad were getting divorced. He had been seeing another woman. And that wasn't all—we had a half-sister on the way.

I was in shock. And for the first time in my life, I hated my dad. In fact, I hated him so much that I couldn't stand to see him. Eventually, my dad moved out and into an apartment with his new "fling." Then he became an alcoholic. Soon it was like I didn't know him anymore.

Address Book

Does an important adult in your life have a drinking problem? **Alateen** is a great organization to help you find ways to cope. Check out their Web site: *www.al-anon.alateen.org* or call to find a meeting near you: **1-888-4AL-ANON**.

CONSIDER THIS . . .

Alcohol affects people's abilities to make good decisions and turns off the "switch" in their brains that helps them **think rationally** and not **act compulsively**. It's no wonder then that most alcoholics find many aspects of their lives disintegrating the more they drink.

A year passed and my dad realized that what he had done was wrong, and he wanted to be back together with my mom. I was furious to say the least, but then my dad went to rehab, and all of a sudden it was like he was a changed man.

And slowly, with time, he did change. My mom and dad are together today, and I love my dad. But when he first came back, all I could think about was how what he did was so wrong and how much it had hurt my family. There was a pain inside of me that I couldn't seem to let go of until I learned I had to forgive my dad. I'll always remember that time in my life, but I know now that everything happens for a reason, even the worst things in life.

When bad things happen, it's okay to be upset and to cry. But it's not okay to let it change you and your life. God forgives me . . . so how could I not forgive my dad?

Mallory Ward, Age 15

For Real?

Trouble at home can have a serious effect on teenagers. Nearly **20%** of teens say they have a difficult family life.

OUTSIDE THE BOX

It's a fact of life . . . everyone gets disappointed sometimes. Whether it's being bummed out over failing a test or losing the big game, or dealing with the devastation of personal disappointment, like when a family comes apart, learning how to handle it when things don't go your way is one of the most important skills you can have. Here are a few tips for handling disappointment:

- Take it easy on yourself, especially if you're feeling down. Do something that makes you feel good about yourself.
- No matter what the situation, try and find some sort of positive way to look at it.
- Know that everyone goes through disappointment, and the feelings that go along with it won't last forever.
- Find a healthy way to express your emotions: Write in your journal, do something creative, go for a walk, talk to someone.
- Try to keep things in perspective. One way to do this is to take the time to write down one thing every day that you are thankful for. It can be something as big as an important person in your life to something as small as the Oreo cookie you had for dessert.

GROWING UP, MY SISTER AND I WEREN'T VERY CLOSE. Even though it was just the two of us and we were only two years apart, for some reason we were constantly at each other's throats, trying to one-up the other or get each other in trouble with our parents. (In fact, this was such a problem that our parents started "fining" us every time one of us tattled. Having to fork over money kind of took the fun out of attempts to get the other one in trouble.)

When my sister left for college, the tattling stopped, and so did most of the conflict. After all, it's hard to get in a fight with your sister when she's 300 miles away. Still, we weren't exactly "close" when things changed and I learned about the true bond of sisterhood.

Seen It?

Sibling rivalry is a classic theme in movies and TV. Have you ever seen any of these movies or TV shows featuring sibling rivalry?

• *The Parent Trap* (1961, 1998)
• *The Incredibles* (2004)
• *Malcolm in the Middle*
• *The Simpsons*

It was a weeknight during my junior year of high school. I was in a deep sleep at about two in the morning when I heard the phone ringing in the kitchen through my bedroom wall. It rang and rang and rang until finally my dad picked it up. A minute later, I heard a light knocking on my door.

"Your sister wants to talk to you," my dad said sleepily.

Huh?

"Me? What does she want?" I answered in shock.

"I don't know. She just asked to talk to you," he said. "And she seemed pretty upset."

I got up and shuffled to the kitchen while my dad went back to bed. When I picked up the phone, my sister broke down and opened up. She was going through a really difficult time at school and had to tell someone what was going on. I couldn't believe that the person she chose to share her pain with was me.

As I lay in bed that night after getting off the phone, I stared at the ceiling, deep in thought. I felt so sad for my sister, so sorry that she was going through a rough time. But I also felt kind of proud, like I had an important responsibility. It took a crisis, but it was a lesson I would never forget—I was a sister, a sibling, a friend.

Open Up

I know there's something wrong
By the look on your face as we
   were on our way home
I have no doubt about this
And by the fact that you can't
   even get the door unlocked
It's taken you at least five min-
   utes to get it open
I want to help so please just open up.

Read It?

Author Sonya Sones presents a collection of poems written from the perspective of a 13-year-old girl who is dealing with her sister's mental break-down in *Stop Pretending: What Happened When My Big Sister Went Crazy.*

In the car you said I was too young and wouldn't
   understand
I might I have been through a lot of stuff
You don't have a clue
And even though I haven't gone through something doesn't
   mean I won't understand
You never know until you start talking
So please just try me and open up.

Sissy, you have always been there for me and you are
   the best ever

Always thinking of me before yourself
Let me take you back
Like when the car windshield
    sprayed glass everywhere
You didn't even worry about yourself
    and if you were hurt
All you wanted to know was that I
    was safe and okay.

For Real?

While having **siblings** has its own baggage, nearly one-third of teens say that they **rely** on their brothers or sisters a lot for **support** and **guidance**.

So now all I want to do is make sure you are okay
All I want is for you to be okay—I'm just looking out for you
Because I hate seeing you hurt the way you are
You won't let me help but I will anyway
You just might not like this help.

Even though you might be mad at me for telling Mom and Dad
You were acting different
Let us help you heal and comfort you
That is what sisters and families are for
So let us do our job.

And I just want you to know even though we don't always
    like each other all the time,
You have a little sister who loves you and is your best friend
If you ever need me I'll be there and if I need you, you'll be
    there, too
I know I can count on you
I just want you to feel the same way
I'm always here for you so don't be afraid.
Open up.

Shelby Coleman, Age 13

OUTSIDE THE BOX

Do you have a sibling or other loved one you want to encourage to open up to you? Here are some ideas for getting them to let you in:

- Be a good listener. Don't interrupt and make sure your loved one knows they have your full attention.
- Share what's going on with you. If your loved one realizes that you trust them with your secrets, maybe they'll trust you in return.
- Don't make judgments. Support your loved one by listening and offering empathy, not a list of "do's" and "don'ts."
- Let your sibling or friend know you're concerned about them.
- Give positive feedback, even if it's just a smile or a hug, to encourage your sibling or friend to continue opening up.

WHERE DO YOU STAND?

How approachable are you?
Do any of these situations resemble how you are at home?

Your bedroom has a "keep out" sign on the door, a double-bolted lock and, if you could, you'd install a security alarm to maintain your privacy.
- THAT'S ME   (0 points)
- SOMETIMES   (1 point)
- NOT ME AT ALL   (2 points)

Eating dinner with the rest of the family might as well be a form of torture. When you're forced to sit at the table, it's never without your iPod blasting music in your ears to drown out everyone else's voices.
- THAT'S ME   (0 points)
- SOMETIMES   (1 point)
- NOT ME AT ALL   (2 points)

You know that your little brother is getting teased at school, but you don't give him the time of day. He needs to deal with these situations on his own, just like you did when you were his age.
- THAT'S ME   (0 points)
- SOMETIMES   (1 point)
- NOT ME AT ALL   (2 points)

You're feeling frustrated about a tough situation you're dealing with at school, but you don't bother going to your parents to talk about it. They don't have a clue about what life is like for you. They'd just never get it.
- THAT'S ME   (0 points)
- SOMETIMES   (1 point)
- NOT ME AT ALL   (2 points)

You know your parents are going through a rough time, especially because they haven't been acting very happy around the house. When they suggest planning a special family vacation for everyone to re-bond, you tell them you can't go and make up an excuse about a big school project.
- THAT'S ME   (0 points)
- SOMETIMES   (1 point)
- NOT ME AT ALL   (2 points)

Add up your points:
    0–3 = You've got a major wall built up.
    4–7 = You usually warm up to the situation.
    8–10 = You're as approachable as they come.

OKAY, I KNOW I JUST TALKED ABOUT HOW MY SISTER
and I got closer after she went away to college, sparked by that
middle-of-the-night phone call. And I wish I could say that things
always stayed this way, but then I'd be lying. There were still times
when my sister and I would say really hateful things to each other,
and the sting would last a long time.

It seems like sometimes we're meaner to the people who love
us because we know they have no choice but to stay in our lives,
while we sometimes show more consideration to perfect strangers
because we don't want to offend them. But when someone in our
family, someone we love, hurls insults our way, the pain can be
much deeper than if the words came from any old acquaintance.
We can internalize the insults and believe they must be true
because they're coming from a trusted source.

The author of this next story learned the hard way how much
power her words had over someone who loved and looked up
to her.

The Turning Point

I stomped out of the house, and the screen door slammed shut behind me. My face was wet with tears. As I started out down the street, I heard my mother call after me, "Dani, take your brother with you." I was in the middle of complete emotional distress, and now my brother was trotting down the driveway behind me. This is exactly why my parents had no idea what was going on. They only talked to me to tell me to take my brother with me or to clean up my room. They had no idea the pain I was enduring.

For Real?

Some animals exhibit serious **sibling rivalry**. Young spotted hyenas will fight with their brothers and sisters for dominance, sometimes to the death. In fact, **25%** of newborn hyenas die because of sibling rivalry.

I walked down the block to my best friend Mike's house. I was going to say good-bye. I didn't want to be here anymore, I couldn't stand that no one understood what I was going through.

Mike opened the door and immediately embraced me in the biggest, tightest hug of my life. My younger brother, whom I had been ignoring, wandered off to play with Mike's brothers.

Mike and I went into his living room to sit down. He didn't ask for an explanation or try to console me; he just held me and let me cry on his shoulder. I sobbed until my sides hurt. I cried about how lonely I was. I cried about how my family didn't seem to understand me at all. And when I was all cried out, I realized that part of the hurt was gone.

It dawned on me that I had been crying and talking with Mike for hours. I called home, and my mother screamed at me for being out past curfew. But instead of picking a fight, I grabbed my brother and started the walk home.

There was something strangely calming about that walk home. Because of this new sense of calm and warmth I was feeling, I decided to tell my brother everything. My brother and I rarely talked, and

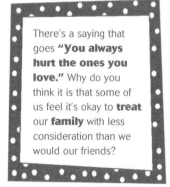

CONSIDER THIS . . .

There's a saying that goes **"You always hurt the ones you love."** Why do you think it is that some of us feel it's okay to **treat** our **family** with less consideration than we would our friends?

when we did, it had only
to do with him tagging
along or arguments over
the remote. But on that
walk home, I spilled my
heart to my sixth-grade
brother, someone I had
never before looked to
for advice or comfort.

For Real?

When you get **upset**, do you
feel better after you've shed a few
tears? There's a **reason why**.
Tears are made up of hormones
and other chemicals that our
brain produces when we get upset.
As we cry, we get rid of the
extra chemicals, thus making
us feel better!

He didn't yell at me or lec-
ture me. He didn't tell me my
feelings were wrong or that I was wrong
for feeling them. He just said, "Please don't die. That would
make me sad." It was then, walking hand-in-hand with my
kid brother, that I decided I wanted to live.

The next day I turned fifteen.

Dani Allred

LIKE IT OR NOT, IT'S OUR PARENTS, *NOT* OUR FRIENDS, who have the biggest impact on who we are as teens and who we become as adults. While friends do have a huge influence on the things we do and the choices we make, at the end of the day it's the people we live with, the people who raise us, who largely shape our personalities, our quirks—even little things like whether or not we put the cap back on the toothpaste. That's because our parents have been "modeling" for us throughout our entire lives. Not "model" like prancing around the room showing off the latest out-of-fashion trends. I mean that our parents' every behavior is what we see and learn from, from the time we're babies, and that behavior is what we grow up thinking is "normal."

Read It?

The book *Make Lemonade* by Virginia Euwer Wolff features 17-year-old LaVaughn who has a chance to turn her life around when her baby-sitter helps her go back to school.

For many of us, our parents' modeling is a good thing. We learn etiquette like saying "please" and "thank you," what we should do in different circumstances, and other important life rules. But what if what's been modeled for us *hasn't* been positive? What if our idea of normal behavior is yelling and hitting or sulking and clamming up? Is it possible to break the cycle?

Yes, it is. But it's not easy. Breaking the cycle of negative or harmful behavior takes a lot of courage and even more willpower. Think about it. There are so many things we do in life that just come naturally to us, but for

CONSIDER THIS . . .

Do you know someone who does things that just seem *odd*? Maybe he acts like a real tough guy all the time, or maybe she lies about the littlest things. This odd behavior might be a form of "acting out," which is when people act a certain way to release negative emotions they might feel about something else.

those who haven't had great influences, even little things might seem like a lot of work and effort. But sometimes all it takes is the help and compassion of one single person to make a difference. When one person believes in you, anything is possible.

Raising Oneself

As a child he was one of the worst I had ever seen
Always demanding the attention of those around him
Never willing to give his own

He never realized the existence
    of morality
Always taking as he pleased
Without asking
Without question

His parents were too busy
Too busy with their own lives
    to see
That their child needed them

No one can be expected
To raise themselves
They need to be taught
What is right
What is wrong

THE WORD

Morals is another word for **rules** about **behavior** that are generally **accepted** by **society** having to do with what's right and what's wrong.

Sadly enough
There are too many children out there
Living without the love
Or guidance
That is needed to coexist with
    others

They'll learn though
Learn the painful way
That people can not be treated like
    trash

It was the first day of school that
    I had met Ryan
He would always sit there
Talking loudly to anyone who
    would listen
He loved to pull my hair
Say mean things to me
Just to see me cry

I hated him

It wasn't until a year later
That we became friends

It was on a cloudy day during the first grade
That I sat outside on the curb waiting for my ride
He was sitting not too far from me
Crying

I had never seen a boy cry before
I didn't know what to do

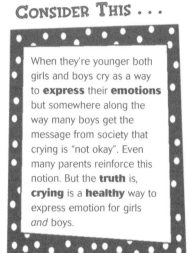

CONSIDER THIS . . .

When they're younger both girls and boys cry as a way to **express** their **emotions** but somewhere along the way many boys get the message from society that crying is "not okay". Even many parents reinforce this notion. But the **truth** is, **crying** is a **healthy** way to express emotion for girls *and* boys.

I just sat
And stared
Finally giving into my sense of guilt
And at a loss for what to do
I got up and walked over to him
I gave him my bag of M&M's
And held him

For Real?
M&Ms were invented in 1940 as a high-energy snack **food** for **soldiers** at war

Since then
He's been the gentlest of hearts

Since then
He's always been there
Been there to comfort me over stupid things that happened
    in life
Whether it be over someone who stole my snack
Whether it be over my family's fighting
Whether it be over the death of a kitten
Whether it be over the loss of my
    eyesight
He's been there

HOW ABOUT YOU?
Have you ever become friends with someone who years earlier you couldn't stand?

Even if high school has distanced
    us
Parted us from seeing one another

I can only hope
That we learn from our parents'
    mistakes
So that we can raise even gentler children
To be as happy as they can be
And kind to others

Delusori Lightning age 17

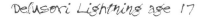

Take the Quiz:

HOW HEALTHY IS YOUR ATTITUDE ABOUT FAMILY LIFE ?

1. Your mom is addicted to the television show *The Amazing Race* and is thrilled when she finds out they're having auditions for their next special family edition. She thinks that you and your family would have the time of their lives racing around the world together. What's your take?

    ___ A. Talk about your worst nightmare come to life, the thought of being stuck with your family for as long as six weeks straight with no break is about as appealing to you as going to the prom naked.

    ___ B. Nonstop time with the fam isn't exactly your idea of a vacation, but the thought of improving your relationship with them doesn't sound all bad.

    ___ C. You've watched *The Amazing Race* and agree with your mom . . . when your family works together, you can do anything! Let's sign up!

2. Your brother is running for class president and needs all the help he can get spreading the word. He asks you to come to school early one day to help him hand out flyers. Are you up for it?

    ___ A. No way! Why should you give up your own personal time for your brother's campaign?

    ___ B. You're kind of embarrassed that your brother is campaigning and you'd rather not get involved, but you compromise by agreeing to help him put up posters after school one afternoon.

_____ C. Even though running for president may not be your thing, you think it's cool that he's so into it and even cooler that he'd come to you for help. You'll be there with a handful of flyers and a smile.

3. Around your house, Sunday nights have always been deemed "game night," but lately you've been feeling like you've outgrown the tradition. What do you do?

_____ A. You gripe and groan every week and make it clear that you're just not into playing games anymore. You figure that if you make your family miserable enough, they'll cut you loose and give you a pardon.

_____ B. You test the waters by skipping out on one night, telling your parents you've got a major paper to finish. If all goes well, you'll lobby to cut down your game-night playing to once or twice a month.

_____ C. You know how important this tradition is to your parents, and actually feel pretty lucky that you have parents who want to stay so involved in your life. Even though you might not announce to the rest of the school that you spend Sunday nights playing Cranium with the folks, you keep your weekly date night.

4. You've never thought twice about having enough money to get what you want until your dad loses his job and suddenly finances are seriously tight around the house. You had been hoping to get a new pair of soccer shoes, and now that plan is in jeopardy. How do you handle it?

_____ A. Your frustration at not being able to get what you want is overwhelming, especially when all of your friends are getting new shoes and you'll be stuck wearing beat-up ones. You sulk around the house and try to guilt your parents into getting the shoes anyway, telling them you can't live without them.

_____ B. You're bummed out about the shoes, but can tell that your folks are feeling strapped. You do a ton of research online and find a wholesaler who sells the shoes at nearly half the cost, and see if your parents can handle that amount.

___ C. You know your parents would get the shoes for you if they could, and you don't want to add any more stress to the money situation than is already there. You decide to hold a yard sale of your old toys and stuff, use the proceeds to buy the shoes, and give any extra to Mom and Dad to help pitch in.

5. You couldn't be more psyched that your class is going on an overnight field trip until you find out that your mom has signed up to be a chaperone. What do you do?

___ A. When pleading and begging with her to reconsider doesn't work, you decide to just ignore your mom while on the trip and make fun of her to the rest of your friends to save face.

___ B. You're fairly horrified that your mom might make some big gaffe and embarrass you, so you keep a low profile and hope that she'll do her own thing and leave you alone.

___ C. While you have to admit that there's a potential for Mom to cramp your style around your friends, you decide to make the best of it and try to discover her fun side now that she's away from Dad and household duties.

Well, how'd you do? Give yourself 30 points for every A, 20 points for every B and 10 points for every C. Look below to find out if you've got a good attitude when it comes to your family:

50–70 points = Sister Sledge's classic song "We Are Family" might as well be your theme song! They might drive you crazy sometimes, but you know your family is a part of you, and you're stuck with them for life. You're a proud member of the team.

80–120 points = You love your family, but you also need more space of your own lately. You wish they'd understand that you're not the same kid you once were, and rebelling from them is just part of what you need to do right now. Keep this in mind . . . a little effort goes a long way. Talk to your folks about your day at the dinner table, and they'll be thrilled that you're letting them in.

130–150 points = You may sleep under the same roof, but as far as you're concerned, your parents couldn't be more unlike you than if they were from a different planet . . . in another galaxy. You might want to make an effort to see things from their perspective and remember that our families are the people who will always be there for us, no matter what.

CHAPTER 4

LOSING IT

Experiencing loss is a part of everyone's life, but everyone experiences it in different ways and at different times. Some of us sail through our youth without ever experiencing a significant loss, while others have to face the loss of a close friend or a parent, or maybe even a threat to their own life. This chapter examines loss and how it affects us, and includes some inspirational stories by teens who turned their loss around and made it a positive event in their lives.

ARE YOU A *GRUDGE-KEEPER?* I used to be. Okay, well, sometimes I still am. But it's something I'm working on. That's because a new friend of mine shared a story with me that has made me think twice about holding grudges.

I was telling my friend how I was upset with one of my relatives because they never called me—it was always me having to call them. So I decided to stop calling them, period. My thinking was that if they wanted to talk with me, they could pick up the phone themselves and show me. And if they didn't, well then, that was just fine with me (even though it really wasn't). When I finished telling my friend the story, I could tell that it had upset her. Then she told me why.

"Yeah, three years ago I was mad at my mom for the same thing, and I played the same game. I stopped calling her. And then she had a stroke and died while I was in the middle of holding a grudge," she said.

Her story stopped me cold. Clearly my friend felt terrible about her stubborn grudge, about wasting time being mad instead of picking up the phone and calling her mom when she wanted to. And now it was too late.

My friend's story has stayed with me to this day, and whenever I feel like playing games or being a grudge-keeper with the people I love, I remember what happened to her, and I choose to act *today*. I hope that this next powerful story stays with you in the same way.

No Day but Today

Webster's *Collegiate Dictionary* defines opportunity as "a favorable juncture of circumstances and a good chance for advancement or progress." These opportunities are great happenings that most people only recognize every once

Seen It?

The hit Broadway musical *Rent* is centered around the theme of "No day but today."

in a while. I, however, see every new day as a blessed opportunity. I have tried to live my life so that I am grateful for each new day, but am not necessarily expecting another. In other words, I live my life by the saying, "No day but today." This lifestyle found its beautiful beginnings in a very dark and depressing time in my life—middle school.

Middle school is a hard time for everyone. The combination of raging hormones, screaming teachers and unforgiving peers is a sure formula for disaster. My formula included a devastatingly unique variable to ensure the toxicity of the outcome. This variable was introduced on a spring evening during sixth grade. As my parents sat my brothers and I down in the living room, they spoke four words that would throw our world into a completely different orbit: "Your father has cancer."

Hearing all of the foreboding statistics terrified my young heart. Wrapping your mind around the

CONSIDER THIS . . .

There is **proof** of the **"power of positive thinking"** and that people who are generally happy tend to live longer and more fulfilling lives. A positive attitude can also help your body **fight disease** and **aging**.

concept of death at age eleven is hard enough, let alone trying to understand why you're being told that your father could die in six months. The helpless feeling only grew as my parents explained that the cancer was a very rare one that didn't respond to chemotherapy. My tears were a raging river of fear, anger and despair that only began to let up as my parents offered words of encouragement. They explained that we were going to make everything all right and that we would fight the cancer with all of our strength. Slightly eased, I walked to my bedroom with my mother and crawled into bed. She helped settle me as she spoke of life and love. After kissing me goodnight, her warm and comforting presence left my room. Soon I gave way to a deep sleep, hoping that I would wake up to a happier reality.

As the months changed and the pages of the calendar flipped, we approached and then surpassed the six-month prediction. My father appeared to lose a pound with every second that passed, but his smile never flickered. Always looking for a laugh, he would make jokes about the tubes and bags coming out of his new man-made orifices. While

---

THE WORD

An **orifice** is an opening into the body, such as the mouth or ears.

---

holding on tightly to his morphine pump and IV pole, he would head-bang right along with the kids to the music playing in our living room. Anyone who came to visit him would always leave happier and more lighthearted than when they arrived. Although his physical strength was rapidly expiring, his spiritual and mental strength only continued to grow.

Fifteen months after that first tear-filled announcement,

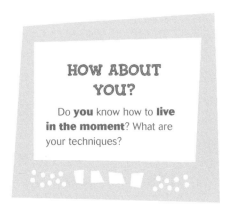

HOW ABOUT YOU?

Do **you** know how to **live in the moment**? What are your techniques?

my father succumbed to the horrific disease that had been slowly taking him. Never one to forget the precious gift of humor, my father was cracking his infamous jokes even on the very day that he took his last breath. Although extremely sad, the day was also full of relief that he could finally be free of pain . . . free of his disease-riddled, sick, earthly body.

The calling hours and funeral were packed with loved ones and friends sharing memories, gratefulness, sympathies and tears. As the dust settled and I finally had a chance to reflect on the life-changing fifteen months I had just gone through, I began to focus on the optimism and love that filled every day, that had become our pillars of strength. We were forced to live every day like it was our last together as a family. We enjoyed every smile, laugh and heartbeat, even through our sadness. We didn't go skydiving, scuba diving or on any extravagant vacations to celebrate our lives . . . we simply loved each other and tied up as many loose ends as possible. We were grateful for each day we had with each other and made sure that there was never any doubt in anyone's heart about the love we shared. This made sleep come easier and helped us to see each new day for the opportunities it brought.

I have yet to come across another notion that has helped

Read It?

Sonya Sones' novel, *One of Those Hideous Books Where the Mother Dies*, deals with the grief of losing a parent from a teen's perspective.

me as much as "No day but today." It opens and defines opportunity to all as the moment of new choices, new advancements and new permission. There is no day but today to *love*. There is no day but today to *accept*. There is no day but today to *listen*. There is no day but today to *live*. Take advantage of every day you are blessed enough to have, and you shall be void of regrets when your days stop coming.

Mary Elizabeth Elsey, Age 18

> ### For Real?
>
> Do you worry about **friends** or family **dying**? If so, you're not alone. **37%** of teens say that death is one of the things they worry about the most.

OUTSIDE THE BOX

Living in the moment, or appreciating every day for what it is, takes <u>practice</u>. Here are some ways to make it a lifelong habit:

- When you find yourself happy, take a moment to sit back and acknowledge what happiness really feels like.
- Recognize it when you see a sight that makes you feel good—leaves turning color in the fall, a happy puppy tripping over its feet, a good friend doubled over in laughter.
- Tell the people you love how you feel about them...there's no time like the present!
- If you find yourself worrying about something that hasn't happened yet or might happen in the future, <u>stop!</u> Stressing over things that are in the future just distracts us from appreciating what we have in the <u>present</u>.

HAVE YOU EVER HEARD OF THE "FIVE STAGES OF GRIEF"? Dr. Elisabeth Kübler-Ross came up with what has become the most common perception of how we all deal with the loss of a loved one. Do any of her five stages of grief sound familiar?

➡ Denial: We don't believe that the loss has happened.
➡ Anger: We are furious with the person who died, with friends, family . . . even the world.
➡ Bargaining: We want to bargain with God to go back in time and have things end differently.
➡ Depression: We are numb and sad about the loss.
➡ Acceptance: We come to accept the loss and stop mourning.

Not everybody experiences all five of these stages, and everyone experiences them differently. Some stages may last only a day while others could last years. And while there is no right or wrong way to handle the deep grief of losing a loved one, there is no doubt that expressing the emotions through writing can be a powerful tool. The author of this next poem writes about the anger she felt after losing her dad.

For Real?
About **1 in 20** teenagers **loses** a **parent** before they turn 18.

I'm No Longer Mad

I'm no longer mad that you didn't try to find me
I'm no longer mad that you died and left without me
I'm no longer mad that you didn't say good-bye
I'm no longer mad, but how come I still cry?

I'm no longer mad because you appear in my dreams telling
    me "hi" and saying that you miss me
I'm no longer mad at the heartache you once caused
I'm no longer mad that you left me without a father
I'm no longer mad because I forgive you for everything.

I now realize that you loved
    me and that you wanted
    to be with me always
So now I'm saying I love you
    too and I'm sorry for
    rejecting you
I'm sorry that you're gone
    and that you just might
    be all alone.

 **Read It?**

If you've lost someone and
are struggling to find a way to
deal with your grief, check out
the book *Straight Talk About
Death for Teenagers: How to
Cope with Losing Someone
You Love* by Earl Grollman.

I'm no longer mad that you didn't try to find me
I'm no longer mad that you died and left without me
I forgive you for everything that happened
Dad, I miss you and I'm no longer mad.

Jasmine Highsmith, Age 16

OUTSIDE THE BOX

If you're dealing with the death of a loved one, here are some strategies for getting a grip on the intense emotions that you might be experiencing:

- Don't keep your emotions inside. Talk to anyone who'll listen about how you're feeling. Getting your feelings out is the first step toward working through them.
- Look for support groups where you can meet other teens who are dealing with the same kinds of things you are. A good place to start is local hospitals.
- Be patient with yourself. You're going through one of the most difficult things anyone in life experiences, and it takes time to heal. At the same time, don't beat yourself up if you're feeling okay quicker than you think you should. There are no rights and wrongs when it comes to dealing with grief.
- Honor the person who's passed on by keeping them alive in your heart. Keep pictures and other keepsakes in an album or memory box . . . something portable and accessible.

FOR MOST OF US, BEING SERIOUSLY ILL, especially when we're young, isn't something we can even fathom; it's so far out of our everyday reality. The sickest I was as a child was a bout of chicken pox and mumps, and I didn't even have those at the same time. I remember being miserable with my itchy pox and swollen cheeks, but I got through it relatively unscathed.

That's why I find this next story, "My Gift of Life," so powerful. The author's incredible attitude and drive for life, even in the midst of the most dire of circumstances—truly a life-and-death situation—is beyond inspiring. It shows me what is really possible . . . how we as people are capable of getting through whatever we might be faced with. I can only hope that I could put on as brave a face as this next author did and continues to do every day.

HOW ABOUT YOU?

Have you ever been **diagnosed** with something **scary**? How did **you** deal?

For Real?

Thousands of newborns end up in the **neonatal intensive care unit** every day as a result of premature birth, low birth weight or other health complications. Each admission to NICU costs thousands of dollars a day.

My Gift of Life

When my mom was pregnant with me, she was told multiple times that I would die within twenty-four hours of birth due to congestive heart failure. They said all she could do was go home and wait until I stopped breathing. So as soon as I came into the world, I was rushed from Norton Hospital, where I was born, to Kosair Children's Hospital in Louisville, Kentucky. Fluid had somehow built up all around my tiny organs, causing severe kidney damage and jeopardizing my life. I spent two weeks in the neonatal intensive care unit. The first year of my life was full of questions without answers for my parents, as well as the first of ten surgeries I would undergo before I reached the age of fifteen.

Let's fast forward a few years. I was eleven and in fifth grade. I'd undergone six surgeries by that time, but the last one was when I was six or seven, so I'd been enjoying time away from being cut open. However, that didn't mean I was okay. My kidneys were slowly failing. In March 2001, I received the news that I needed a kidney transplant. The only problem was I needed one last major surgery before I could even be put on the national waiting list to get a kidney. I was scared. Memories of my past haunted me. I didn't want to go through the pain again. I only told my closest friends what was happening because I was embarrassed by the whole

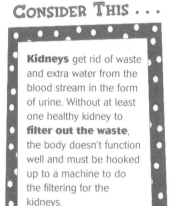

CONSIDER THIS . . .

Kidneys get rid of waste and extra water from the blood stream in the form of urine. Without at least one healthy kidney to **filter out the waste**, the body doesn't function well and must be hooked up to a machine to do the filtering for the kidneys.

situation. Word got out soon enough, however, and I was both blessed and surprised when, the Friday before my surgery, my class presented me with a pillowcase that they had all signed.

On April 30, 2001, I underwent my last major operation before transplantation at Riley Children's Hospital in Indianapolis, Indiana. This was my hardest surgery by far—both physically and emotionally. During my two-week stay at Riley, I was visited by friends, family, church members and even my teacher, who brought me cards that my classmates had made. I remember crying when I realized it was Mother's Day and that my mom was stuck in the hospital with me. Needless to say, I was ecstatic when I was allowed to go home.

For Real?

More than 80,000 people in the U.S. are on the national waiting list for an **organ transplant**, with more than 55,000 waiting for kidneys. Every day, approximately 63 people have an organ transplant, while 16 die because they didn't receive the organ they needed in time.

The summer that followed was filled with bittersweet emotions. On the one hand, I was happy. I had made a huge comeback after three weeks of hospitalization in order to lead my softball team to their first two wins of the season, earn myself a game ball and snag a spot on the All-Star Team. On the other hand, I was scared. My kidney specialists in Louisville told my parents and me that I had only 10 percent kidney function. I tried to keep a brave face, but inside I was being torn apart. I had been told that I wouldn't make it to Christmas.

Dialysis surgery was scheduled for July 23, 2001, in the

hope that it would help me make it through middle school. The search for a donor began. Both of my parents were tested, but neither one of them was a match. All four of my siblings were too young, so extended family, church members, friends and people I didn't even know who cared were all tested, but no one was a match. I tried to pretend like nothing was happening. The week before the scheduled surgery, I played two softball games for my All-Star Team, both of which we won.

The day before the surgery, I asked my mom when we'd start packing. She surprised me by saying we weren't going to the hospital—my surgery had been postponed to August 8. I don't remember much about those few weeks. All I remember is Mom and Dad crying and talking on the phone a lot. I was later informed a potential donor had been found, which was the reason behind the postponement, but extensive testing revealed a small kidney stone in my donor's kidney, therefore abruptly stopping the process. However, because of

> **For Real?**
>
> Getting a **kidney** from a **live donor** can be better than from a nonliving donor because it usually starts working as soon as it's placed in its new body.

God's grace, she was finally cleared to donate. The transplant surgery was rescheduled for the last time. I was happy to know that on August 30, 2001, I'd get my gift of life.

On August 29, my parents, the kidney donor and I drove to University Hospital in Indianapolis for admitting. The next morning I got up at 5:30 A.M. for one final blood test. By 6:00 A.M., I was sitting in the doorway of my hospital room in a wheelchair waiting to be taken to the operating room to prep for my transplant. As I waited, I started to doze off when I saw the donor across the hall. She was in a wheelchair, too. As the nurses came to take us our separate ways, we gave each other the thumbs-up sign. I knew everything would be okay. The donor went home only four days after the operation, while I stayed in the hospital for a week. I went home the day before my twelfth birthday. Believe me, it was an *awesome* birthday present!

Now, four years later, not a single day goes by that I don't thank God for my life. It's a gift to be enjoyed, embraced and cherished. It is opportunities waiting to be grabbed, memories waiting to be made and dreams waiting to be chased. Don't let life slip away—grab it with both fists—because once it's gone, you can never grab it back.

Sarah Beesing, Age 16

OUTSIDE THE BOX

Being stuck in the hospital for an extended period of time can be really tough and boring. Here are some survival tips for a hospital stay:

- Ask the nurses to introduce you to other teens on the floor.
- Have your parents bring you a favorite T-shirt or pair of slippers that reminds you of home and shows off your style.
- Watch DVDs that make you laugh.
- Ask friends to visit often!
- Go for walks, especially outside, if you can.
- Ask for a laptop to log on and IM with your friends.

WHERE DO YOU STAND?

Can you cope with being sick or injured?
Answer the following questions to find out.

When you wake up in the morning feeling under the weather, you . . .

• mope and moan and get back in bed.   (0 points)

• tell your parents you're not well and get their opinion.   (1 point)

• drink fluids, take a shower and see if you feel any better.   (2 points)

If you had to stay in the hospital for a few weeks, you would . . .

• go absolutely crazy.   (0 points)

• be totally bummed out.   (1 point)

• focus on getting better.   (2 points)

You wipe out big-time while skateboarding and scrape your hand enough to draw blood. You . . .

• panic and have your friend rush you to the emergency room. (0 points)

• stop riding your board, afraid of further injury.   (1 point)

• wash out your hand and assess the damage.   (2 points)

You broke your right arm in gym class, and you're stuck in a cast for two months. You . . .

• can't stand it.   (0 points)

• find a way to cope.   (1 point)

• challenge yourself to learn how to write with your left hand.   (2 points)

The hospital has to shave part of your head to give you stitches you need after suffering a fall. You . . .

• hide out until your hair grows back.   (0 points)

• keep a low profile.   (1 point)

• take the opportunity to try out some wacky wigs.   (2 points)

Add up your points:
   0–3 = Being sick or injured is your worst nightmare.
   4–7 = You manage to find a way to get through.
   8–10 = You make the best out of any situation.

Spotlight On... WHEN YOU'RE THE ONE WHO'S SICK

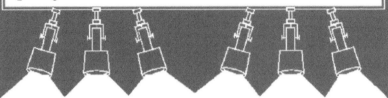

For most of us, a bad cold or the flu is the extent of our experience with being sick. But for some teens, being sick is just a part of daily life. For those teens with chronic illness, or illness that is ongoing, day-to-day life can be a struggle. Some of the more common chronic illnesses among teens are things like:

- diabetes
- asthma
- lupus
- Marfan Syndrome
- cancer
- Chronic Fatigue Syndrome

Teens with chronic illness struggle with the same kinds of things as regular teens, but for them, the feelings can be even more intense. Here are just a few of the challenges these teens face:

- Body image issues—Because chronic illness can sometimes affect the way a person looks, teens with chronic illness tend to be extra concerned about wanting to look just like everyone else.

- Independence issues—Parents of chronically ill children are often overprotective, while at the same time, these teens might be extra attached to the safety and security of their family.
- Friendship issues—Because some of these teens are in and out of the hospital, making and keeping friends can be tough.

According to KidsHealth (*www.kidshealth.org*), the best way for chronically ill teens to cope is to acknowledge that they are different, learn more about their illness, get involved in making decisions on how to treat it, and be aware of the fact that other kids might treat them differently.

Address Book

To find out more info about organ donation and registration, check out the teen organization, Student Donor, online at *www.studentdonor.org*.

LIFE AS WE KNOW IT REALLY CAN CHANGE IN AN INSTANT, whether as the result of something we do or say or the actions of someone else . . . even as a reaction to nature itself.

When change is thrust upon us unwillingly, it can be really difficult to cope. We find ourselves doing the "what ifs." *What if I had done this differently? What if she had said this? What if he had done that?*

While the "what ifs" are a natural reaction to a sudden turn of events, there is really no more useless thing to do to ourselves. Because no matter how much we want to, we can't turn back time. And while we can't go back and change the past, we can take comfort in knowing that the present will always change. And the future really is in our hands.

Read It?

Tears of a Tiger by Sharon Draper tells the story of a boy struggling with his role in the drunken-driving death of his best friend.

A Broken Fence

It was as normal a day as any
When I walked out to the shed
I put the key in the ignition
And the helmet on my head

I backed out very slowly
Then drove into the back field
The tires hit the pavement
And the four-wheeler slowly stopped

I knocked upon the wooden frame
Of my best friend's front door
She put on her helmet, then held on tight
As I sped up a little more

We laughed and bumped atop the machine
Then tried to slow down for a stop
I hit the throttle instead of the brake
And over a hill we flew

My friend's helmet flew off going over the hill
And mine when we hit the fence
She fell off and was lying still by a bush
I leaned beside her, this not making sense

Only five minutes later the ambulance came
And I wasn't allowed to go with her
I was scared for her life when tears filled my eyes
I realized then it was too late

She'd escaped death's grip but the damage was done
And it should have been me instead
Standing here today I look sadly her way
As we stand by the broken fence

Heather Steadman, Age 15

OUTSIDE THE BOX

Feelings of guilt can be some of the hardest to face, especially when we're in some way responsible for accidentally hurting someone else. Here are some strategies for coping with feelings of guilt:

- Remember that it was an accident. Realize that if you knew someone would get hurt, you would have done things differently.
- Apologize to anyone and everyone you need to in order to move on. Even if they don't forgive you, you'll know that you did and said everything you could.
- Try to resume a sense of normalcy in areas of your life where you can, and don't beat yourself up for being happy. Being miserable won't change the past.
- Most importantly, learn to forgive yourself. The only person who can truly help you get over your feelings of guilt is you. _Remember_ . . .you're only human, and you're allowed to make mistakes. We all do.

CONSIDER THIS . . .

Helmets only **protect** us if they fit right. A good helmet should stay snug to the head even when you shake it all around. If you can remove the helmet without pulling it out at the sides, it's probably too big.

READER/CUSTOMER CARE SURVEY

We care about your opinions! Please take a moment to fill out our online Reader Survey at **http://survey.hcibooks.com**. As a **"THANK YOU"** you will receive a **VALUABLE INSTANT COUPON** towards future book purchases as well as a **SPECIAL GIFT** available only online! Or, you may mail this card back to us and we will send you a copy of our exciting catalog with your valuable coupon inside. (PLEASE PRINT IN ALL CAPS)

First Name   MI.   Last Name

Address   City

State   Zip   Email

1. Gender
- ❏ Female
- ❏ Male

2. Age
- ❏ 8 or younger
- ❏ 9-12
- ❏ 13-16
- ❏ 17-20
- ❏ 21-30
- ❏ 31+

3. Did you receive this book as a gift?
- ❏ Yes
- ❏ No

4. How did you find out about the book?
- ❏ Friend
- ❏ School
- ❏ Parent
- ❏ Online
- ❏ Store Display
- ❏ Teen Magazine
- ❏ Interview/Review

5. Where do you usually buy books?
(please choose one)
- ❏ Bookstore
- ❏ Online
- ❏ Book Club/Mail Order
- ❏ Price Club (Sam's Club, Costco's, etc.)
- ❏ Retail Store (Target, Wal-Mart, etc.)

6. What magazines do you like to read? *(please choose one)*
- ❏ Teen People
- ❏ Seventeen
- ❏ YM
- ❏ Cosmo Girl
- ❏ Rolling Stone
- ❏ Teen Ink
- ❏ Christian Magazines

7. What books do you like to read? *(please choose one)*
- ❏ Fiction
- ❏ Self-help
- ❏ Reality Stories/Memoirs
- ❏ Sports
- ❏ Series Books (Chicken Soup, Fearless, etc.)

8. What attracts you most to a book?
(please choose one)
- ❏ Title
- ❏ Cover Design
- ❏ Author
- ❏ Content

TAPE IN MIDDLE; DO NOT STAPLE

BUSINESS REPLY MAIL

FIRST-CLASS MAIL PERMIT NO 45 DEERFIELD BEACH, FL

POSTAGE WILL BE PAID BY ADDRESSEE

Chicken Soup for the Soul® (Teens)
3201 SW 15th Street
Deerfield Beach FL 33442-9875

FOLD HERE

Books for Life

Do you have your own Chicken Soup story
that you would like to send us?
Please submit at: **www.chickensoup.com**

Comments

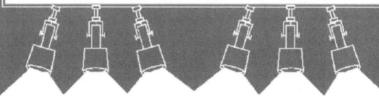

Spotlight On . . .
WHEN TRAGEDY STRIKES

Senseless accidents are so difficult to deal with because so many of us are looking for answers to the question of *WHY? Why is this happening to me? Why did it have to happen at all? Why can't I go back and do things differently? Why does the rest of my life have to be different now?*

While it's true that after experiencing a tragedy in your life you might never be quite the same person you were before, this doesn't always have to be a bad thing. Maybe the changes that you go through will end up being ones that define who you are. Maybe they'll even make you *stronger*.

If you're trying to come to terms with a tragedy in your life, these tips might get you on the road to recovery:

- Holding on to negative feelings is like asking the flu virus to stick around just because you like to feel sick. Get those feelings out in a healthy way: Go for a run, shoot hoops, dive into a book, cry, laugh, journal . . . you get the idea.
- Look for support—in friends, family, support groups, books. You need as many tools as possible

to help you get through this rough time, and if you start looking, you'll find that support really is everywhere.

- Take the time every day to do something nice for yourself, whether it's relaxing in front of the tube or going window-shopping. If you can experience a few minutes of happiness here and there where you can actually distract yourself from what's going on, you'll find that as the days and weeks go by, you'll spend more and more time being happy.

- Be patient with yourself and realize that it might take a while to start feeling like you again.

TRY THIS EXPERIMENT. Open up your journal or find a piece of paper and jot down the names of your three closest friends. Now think about the time when you first met them. Did you connect instantly? What were your first impressions? Do you remember what he or she was wearing? Did you make any assumptions based on how they looked? And if so, did your assumptions turn out to be wrong?

If you're like most people, your list contains at least one name of someone you initially didn't see yourself being friends with. That's because people are like onions—we all have many different layers. And if you don't take the time to peel away the skin, you might never get to the juicy layers underneath.

Chain Reaction

One year ago, I was a normal student in high school. I was just about to start my senior year, and as the weeks before school approached unbelievably fast, I was dreading another year. I was nobody special. I made okay grades, I didn't hang out with the "in" crowd, and I was guilty of making terrible first judgments about people and never giving them second chances. I was even guilty of making fun of a few people who weren't as well off as I was. I was mean and cruel. As the first day of the school year started, I had no idea how much one person would change my life forever.

HOW ABOUT YOU?

Do you ever make **snap judgments** only to find out later that you couldn't have been more **wrong**?

I first met Ashley in my third-period English class on the first day of school. She sat next to me and looked as if she hadn't washed her clothes in years. Her hair was in knots and her shoes were covered in holes. I had a terrible first impression of her, and I wanted nothing to do with this girl. Then during the second week of school, we were given projects to do with a partner. Our assignment was to find out everything we could about the other person and write a five-page bio about them. When the

CONSIDER THIS . . .

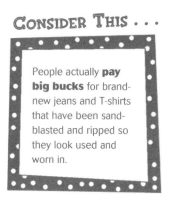

People actually **pay big bucks** for brand-new jeans and T-shirts that have been sand-blasted and ripped so they look used and worn in.

Read It?

Jerry Spinelli's novel *Loser* is about an interesting guy who everyone gets wrong.

teacher read the names of our partners, I was disturbed to find out that I had to work with Ashley. The worst part was that we would have no class time to work on it. It was all to be done outside of school. *Great.*

I was to go to Ashley's house after school that day to begin the project. When I arrived, I was surprised to see her house. It was bigger than mine. So why did she look as if she had no home? I was very confused. Her family seemed very nice and welcomed me into their home with open arms. As the night went on, I was surprised to find out that Ashley was actually a lot like me. We liked the same music, had the same hobbies, and she was the middle child of an older brother and a younger sister, just like I was. I felt terrible for judging her so quickly based on her looks.

HOW ABOUT YOU?

Have you ever thought about what your **lifetime goal** is?

Then, when we got to a question for the assignment, "What is your biggest lifetime goal?" she gave me an answer that left me speechless.

"My goal is to start a chain reaction of kindness. I want to

Seen It?

In the movie *Pay It Forward* (2000), Haley Joel Osment plays a boy who hopes his actions spur a chain reaction of kindness.

make people in the world feel good about themselves and I want people to stop making fun of those who are less fortunate than they are. Once someone shows a little kindness, it will rub off on everyone else and start a chain reaction," she explained.

I felt as if she was directing her answer right at me. After that day, Ashley and I became the best of friends. She showed me a lot about life and taught me to be a better person. I started giving people around me the second chances that they deserved. Ashley was so carefree and lived life to the fullest, always worrying about helping others before helping herself. I felt so thankful that I had this wonderful person in my life.

For Real?

41% of high school freshmen and **87%** of high-school seniors **have jobs**, either during the school year or over the summer.

Two weeks before graduation, my car broke down, and I had no way to get to work. My job was five miles away, and if I missed one more day, my boss was going to let me go. So I called Ashley, and she told me I could take her car because her job was within walking distance from her house. I hesitated at first, but she insisted because that's the type of person she was. Thankfully, I made it to work on time.

That night, Ashley left her job at around 9:00 P.M. and should've arrived at home within five minutes. I was waiting at her house with her car, but she never made it there.

THE WORD

A **legacy** is something that is passed down from someone in the past. If you want to record your legacy so it can be passed down, it's never too early. Check out Duane Elgin and Coleen Ledrew's book, *Living Legacies: How to Write, Illustrate and Share Your Life Stories.*

On her way home, Ashley was mugged. A witness said that the mugger told her if she gave him her wallet, she would be fine. He lied. He shot and killed her right there. Not one day has gone by that I haven't blamed myself for what happened. If I hadn't taken her car, Ashley would still be here today. But her mother helped me realize that she was just doing what she did best—helping another with her kindness.

At her funeral, I promised Ashley that I would keep her goal of a chain reaction alive. I would spread all the kindness that I could on to others in need and tell them to do the same so her name will never be forgotten. My life was saved because of one person, and I thank God every day that he brought her into my life.

Megan Leigh, Age 19

THERE'S NO WAY AROUND IT—dealing with the death of a close friend is one of the most difficult things we'll go through in our lives. And when it happens to someone so young, it brings up all kinds of questions. Questions about why it happened, what death really means, what happens after we die, and on and on. There are no clear answers, and many of us hang on to our faith or belief in God to help us make sense of it all. It's helpful to remember that even though someone has passed on, their imprint has been made on the Earth.

Every person that our friend came into contact with will feel a loss on some level, and hopefully this loss will turn into something positive. Maybe it will make someone cherish the little things in life, or it will encourage someone to follow their dreams today instead of waiting for the future. And even though it can be hard to make sense of the death of someone so young, thinking about all of the good your friend set into motion brings comfort.

The Day an Angel Was Made

I lost my best friend when I was in fifth grade, and it was the worst thing I've ever gone through. I remember waiting for her to come to class one Monday morning, and she just never showed up. I had just arrived at school and was waiting for Devon to get off the bus so I could tell her what had happened to me over the weekend, but I soon found out that Devon's weekend had been much worse. My other close friend, Shayln, arrived at school red-faced and teary.

Read It?

The novel *Elsewhere* by Gabrielle Zevin tells the story of 15-year-old Liz Hall and her experiences in the afterworld after she dies on her way to the mall.

She said two words I was completely unprepared for: "Devon died." It took my breath away, and suddenly my eyes flooded with tears. Shayln just hugged me. We cried together and talked about all the fun times that we'd had with Devon.

The weekend before, Devon and her family had gone camping at Navajo Lake in the southwestern part of Colorado. Devon and her older brother decided to take a walk along the edge of a cliff. They were messing around and picking on each other like brothers and sisters do when all of a sudden water rushed up on them from the canyon below. The water seemed to grab hold of the mud and dirt and yank it out from under their feet, sending them both into the water. They tried grasping for something to hang onto, but all they found was each other's hands. Devon's brother tried with all of his might to hang on to his frightened sister's hand, but there was nothing he could do—her hand was too slippery. He tried over and over again to retrieve the grip, but he couldn't hang on to her—the current and the pressure of the water pulling her farther and farther from his reach was too much. He ran for help, but by the time he returned, Devon had been swept down the mud-filled canyon and drowned.

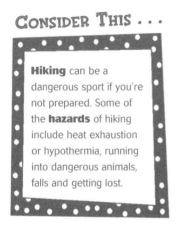

CONSIDER THIS . . .

Hiking can be a dangerous sport if you're not prepared. Some of the **hazards** of hiking include heat exhaustion or hypothermia, running into dangerous animals, falls and getting lost.

The funeral followed a few days later. Devon's small white body was lying limp in the casket with her golden hair lying gently across her shoulders. She seemed so peaceful. She had left the world of problems and hate to enter a world of love and beauty. As I looked upon her face, I imagined what she was doing and wondered if she was seeing the loving eyes of God. I knew that everything was all right, but it would never be the same. I would never again get to hear Devon's cheerful laugh or see her bright blue eyes glistening in the recess sun. Never again would I get to run and play with her in the field, teasing the boys. All I had to remember her by was a torn photo and my memories of a lifetime we had experienced together.

During the ceremony of remembrance, I looked at Devon and wondered how she felt not being able to move, blink or even breathe. We sang all of the songs that she used to sing on the bus or during recess. Something made me want to kiss her ice-cold cheeks and hold her and tell her everything was all right. The thing I will remember the most about her is the way that she made me laugh when I was around her. Devon never once let the smile upon her face turn into a frown.

HOW ABOUT YOU?

Do you keep someone's **memory alive** by talking with them?

Six years have slowly passed, and not a day goes by that I don't think of her. After Devon first left me, I used to go to her spot in the graveyard. I would sit there and cry and ask her to please help me overcome what had happened. I knew that she wasn't there, but her loving and caring spirit will always stay in my heart. I know that if ever I feel the need to talk to her, she is just a voice away. Devon had a passion for life that I've never seen in a person before. She was a blessing to all who knew her. I am so very proud to say that she was my best friend. She lived her life one day at a time and never took anything for granted. Rest in peace, my dear friend.

Mackenzie Manfrom, Age 17

OUTSIDE THE BOX

The act of making a memory book can be useful in coming to terms with the death of a friend, and will also be a wonderful keepsake that you'll always be glad you have. Here are some things to include in your memory book:

- Photos of you and your friend together
- Ticket stubs, receipts, notes and other scraps that have significance to you
- Words or phrases that your friend used to say all the time
- Lyrics to your friend's favorite songs
- Handwritten stories about the two of you, your favorite memories

I'M A BIT OF A CONTROL FREAK—towels must be folded a certain way, and if something doesn't go like I think it should, I feel compelled to make things right. Likewise, when someone I care about deeply is doing things that I am worried about, I want to "fix them" with all my will.

And it took trying to "fix" a friend with a drinking problem, and failing *miserably*, for me to realize that I just have to let go of some things. Some things are just beyond my control. Probably the hardest

For Real?

Drinking alcohol as a teen might seem like a rite of passage, but would you believe that the age at which you start drinking could impact your future? Research shows that teens who try their first drink under the age of 15 are **four times** as likely to have a **drinking problem** as adults.

lesson for me to learn was that letting go doesn't mean that you don't care about someone anymore. It's just realizing that the only person you really have any control over is yourself. You can still be supportive without holding someone's hand and taking their steps for them. And this lesson is one that the author of this next story, "My Star Girl," learned when she had to do some letting go of her own.

My Star Girl

I hung up the white cordless phone and sat cross-legged on the edge of my bed, running my fingers through the fringe of my dark blue chenille blanket.

I had just gotten off the phone after having a long, tearful conversation with my old friend Elyse. Elyse had just gotten out of rehab. She now only had to see her parole officer twice a week and get drug-tested twice a month. She told me she was doing better now, and felt she had weathered the worst of the storm.

For Real?
The first **cordless telephone** was used in 1980, and had a range of less than 100 feet!

Elyse and I met in high school concert band the first week of ninth grade. She played a squeaky black clarinet, and I played a shiny silver flute. She was different from the miniskirt divas I usually encountered. She was unique.

CONSIDER THIS . . .

If **outcasts** find each other and become friends, are they still outcasts?

She had hot pink streaks in her dark brown hair, triple-pierced ears and dark blue toenails. Personally, I always thought she looked gorgeous when she put on a black dress and heels. She had sparkling brown eyes and a gentle sprinkling of freckles over her tanned shoulders and arms. On the rare occasion she laughed, it was light and airy, like flower petals floating in the wind.

HOW ABOUT YOU?

When you're **feeling stressed** out or **unhappy**, what calms you down?

We were both outcasts. I was the quiet introvert who sat alone during lunch and read fantasy novels. I was never too skilled at keeping and making friends; I found most girls too fake and artificial to get along with.

Elyse had a past. Her mom was an alcoholic and addicted to drugs when she was born. Her ex-military father tried to raise her the best he could, but when he remarried his attention shifted from his daughter to his pretty new wife. Elyse never got along with her stepmom, who was more concerned with parenting her cute six-year-old daughter. Sometimes when I was on the phone, I could hear the two of them arguing, screaming things so terrible that I had to muffle the receiver.

For Real?

Even though most states have laws that say teens under 18 years of age must have a parent's permission to get a **tattoo**, **10%** of teens have them. The average age teens get their first tattoo is 14 years old.

Elyse loved the stars. She had one tattooed on her hip—a

blood red shooting star outlined in black. She had a telescope in her room, and when I slept over at her house we would sneak outside well after midnight and sit on turquoise and yellow beach towels on her back lawn and look up into the sky. The comfortable darkness enveloped us, and we would gaze, fascinated, at the silver sparkling orbs above.

Looking out of my bedroom window that night after our phone conversation, I saw that there were stars in the sky. They seemed dull, as though they somehow lacked

 **Seen It?**

In the cult classic *Less Than Zero* (1987), Robert Downey Jr. plays a recent high-school grad who develops an out-of-control drug problem, much to his best friend's dismay.

something. Maybe they just seemed so far away, like a distant memory clinging to the edges of my mind.

Elyse may as well have been up there with the stars for all the distance that had come between us since those precious years of innocence. Two and a half years after we had become close friends, Elyse's stepmom decided she wanted a more extravagant house. And so Elyse and her family moved three towns over, about forty-five minutes from where she used to live.

The move changed her. I still don't know what happened—something inside of her just snapped. Thrown into a new town with the expectation of getting along with new people, she just couldn't handle it.

When our nightly two-hour phone conversations dwindled to brief "hellos" once a week, I knew she had started smoking pot again. I also knew with an absolute certainty that she was hurting and alone, but there was nothing I could do. I was forced to sit there and watch my best friend in the world fall apart before my eyes.

Five months after Elyse moved away, her stepmom called me late one Thursday night in a state of panic. Elyse had run away from home, and none of her friends had any idea where she was.

She had gone back to California to live with her twenty-year-old cousin. When the cops located her and brought her back to Arizona two weeks later, she found herself in a world of problems. She had been drinking every night, smoking marijuana multiple times a day, and even experimenting with more hardcore drugs.

Elyse was admitted to a rehab program that week, at seventeen years of age.

Losing a friend is never easy, but watching them waste away before your eyes is even harder. Throughout all of Elyse's struggles, I kept watching her get hurt, and I felt guilty. I always thought there had to be something that I should have done.

Sadly, there wasn't. Sometimes there's nothing we can do when a friend takes a turn down the wrong path. Elyse simply had to find her own solution to her problems. I think she did, eventually, but something happened to her in the process. The Elyse I know now is not the girl I used to be best friends with—that Elyse is gone forever. But for as long as the night sky continues to shine bright, I will never forget my star girl.

Amy Abbott, Age 17

WHERE DO YOU STAND?

Can you recognize it when one of your friends is in trouble? How would you approach these situations?

Your BFF starts getting text messages that she hides from you. She's acting more secretive to boot.

- NONE OF MY BUSINESS   (0 points)
- KEEP AN EYE OPEN   (1 point)
- GET INVOLVED   (2 points)

Your friend shows up at a school dance acting all weird, and you're sure you smell alcohol on his breath.

- NONE OF MY BUSINESS   (0 points)
- KEEP AN EYE OPEN   (1 point)
- GET INVOLVED   (2 points)

Your study buddy suddenly isn't interested in prepping for tests anymore, and you notice her grades have taken a nosedive.

- NONE OF MY BUSINESS   (0 points)
- KEEP AN EYE OPEN   (1 point)
- GET INVOLVED   (2 points)

You've noticed that your friend is wasting away and acting especially withdrawn lately.

- NONE OF MY BUSINESS   (0 points)
- KEEP AN EYE OPEN   (1 point)
- GET INVOLVED   (2 points)

You used to know every last detail about your friend and her significant other, but suddenly she's keeping her mouth shut about what's going on. She's not acting especially happy either.

- NONE OF MY BUSINESS   (0 points)
- KEEP AN EYE OPEN   (1 point)
- GET INVOLVED   (2 points)

Add up your points:

   0–3 = You don't like to get involved in other people's problems.
   4–7 = You give your friend the benefit of the doubt, but would jump in
         if something major happened.
   8–10 = You're seriously tuned in and you want to be involved in your
          friends' lives.

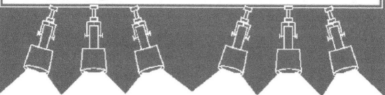

Spotlight On . . . CODEPENDENCY

When people have friends with serious problems like alcoholism and other diseases, it's all too easy to become *codependent*. The urge to try and solve your friends' problems or do everything you can to make them happy is strong. To make matters worse, oftentimes the people with the serious problems make their friends feel guilty, therefore encouraging them to give their all.

But don't be fooled. When you focus so much on the way other people behave or what they need that *you* start to neglect how *you* feel and what *you* need, that's being codependent. It isn't good for you, and being codependent can actually make someone else's problems worse by not encouraging them to deal with their problems on their own.

Do you act codependent with a friend who has a problem? Do you:
- Feel responsible for your friend's behavior?
- Put more into the relationship than most people would?
- Depend on your relationship too much?
- Feel afraid of being alone?

Helping friends through a problem is a great thing to do, as long as it doesn't take over your life. Remember, the only person you have any power over is yourself. Don't take responsibility for somebody else's life!

OUTSIDE THE BOX

If you're worried about how a friend is acting and you want to get involved, here are some tips for approaching your friend:

- Let your friend know that you want to talk with him or her and then set aside time rather than dropping the bomb on your friend when they're least expecting it. You don't want to start off the conversation by putting your friend on the defensive.
- Don't <u>judge</u> your friend. Just let them know that you're concerned, and most of all that you love them and want to help if you can.
- Don't be hurt if your friend gets angry with you for intervening. Sometimes hearing the truth can be a difficult thing.
- Don't just tell your friend that what they're doing concerns you. Tell them how it affects you and exactly why you're worried.
- Let your friend know that you're there for him or her, no matter what.

FOR AMERICANS IN THE EASTERN PART of the United States, hurricanes are a part of life. Every year from June 1 through November 30, hurricane season churns along, and a handful of storms make landfall and create havoc for the people affected. But Hurricane Katrina was no ordinary hurricane, and the aftermath was like nothing witnessed in this country for more than a hundred years.

For Real?
Hurricane Katrina is the third **deadliest storm** to hit the United States since 1900.

Most of us stood by and helplessly watched the images on our TV screens—rising floodwaters, floating cars, thousands of refugees, stranded people and animals, homes ripped from their foundation. But for those who were directly impacted by the storm, the images are much more vivid. And even though it's now been months since that storm violently collided with Louisiana and Mississippi, those affected, among them thousands of teenagers, are still picking up the pieces and trying to rebuild their lives. This next story, "An Unforgettable Storm," is written by one such teen.

An Unforgettable Storm

Nothing in my life has ever compared to this. This one, single day has forever changed my life—even now I can still feel the fright and misery. I know I'm not alone—Hurricane Katrina has caused many others the same pain I feel. It has cost me almost everything dear to my heart—my loved ones, my belongings . . . my home. I will never forget this traumatizing experience.

HOW ABOUT YOU?

Has your life ever been **impacted** by a **natural disaster**?

As I lay there on the hard floor in darkness, I was awakened by the whistling wind trying to ram its way into my mother's store in Uptown, New Orleans. I stood up trying my best to not make a sound so I wouldn't wake the others from their slumber of hope.

Finding my mother and my stepfather already awake because of the hungry wind, I invited myself to sit next to them as they talked with one another. They spoke words that described their lives back in Vietnam. My stepfather walked over and turned up the volume on the TV to override the sounds of my grandfather's monstrous snoring. As we watched the newscast predict what the aftermath of the hurricane would be like, the lights and electronics shut off in unison.

I walked over to the window and stared at the hissing wind dancing with the rain. I remember thinking, *What's going to happen after this? Will we be saved? Will things be back to the way they were? Where will our lives go from here?* Even today my heart ponders these thoughts.

> ### For Real?
> The **destruction** of **Hurricane Katrina** wasn't just caused by rising floodwaters. There were 36 tornadoes that came through with the hurricane, hitting Mississippi, Georgia, Alabama, Pennsylvania and Virginia.

Read It?

The YA novel *Galveston's Summer of the Storm* by Julie Lake is historical fiction about the 1900 Hurricane in Galveston, Texas, as seen through the eyes of a 14-year-old girl.

One by one, my family members woke up and joined me at the window as the hurricane passed. We watched windows and doors get torn off from the other stores around us. To my surprise, it wasn't as bad as I thought it would be. I thought the hurricane would just pick us up and blow us away like trash. In fact, it wasn't scary until right after we picked up our blankets and pillows. That's when the water started to seep in. We rushed to save the products in the store that could be damaged, moving everything onto higher shelves.

For Real?

Tens of thousands of **people left Louisiana** and **Mississippi**, refugees in their own country. Today, they are scattered across all fifty states, and nearly **50%** of them say they **don't intend to go back** to their hometown.

The water came up to my calves. At first the water was really clear, but it soon became murky, probably from the nasty stuff in the sewers. It was terrifying and tiresome.

After what seemed like hours of brushing water out of the store, we finally got our things together and got ready to leave New Orleans. As we tried to leave, we found out quickly that we were trapped by water, which blocked our way to escape, so we came back to my mother's store. With nothing to do, we just sat around and tried to get things ready for another night's rest from all the fear. Before we went to sleep, we stood outside looking up at the pitch-black sky. I remember it was so clear out that we could see every star there. As we talked, we closed the main entrance, said our good nights and found ourselves laying on the cold, hard, harsh floor . . . *again*.

The next thing I remember, I felt a bright light hitting my eyes, which caused me to wake up in wonder. *Is everyone still alive?* I thought, knowing that we could have died in our sleep from carbon-monoxide poisoning. *Did we make it through another night?*

BANG! BANG! We heard a loud knocking at the door.

"Hey, are you guys open? Are you guys gonna sell any-thing?" a man asked my very pregnant mother.

"No, no, we are closed. We're not selling anything. Sorry," my mother replied in her thick accent.

"What? Well, if you're not selling, then I suggest you guys get out!" the man shouted to us.

I walked out and gave the man a questioning look. "Why should we flee?" I asked.

The man grabbed my arm and pointed down the street. "The pipes that are supposed to pump the floodwater into the ocean got jammed. All the water is coming back in!" he replied.

I stood there in shock as I saw that the water was indeed rising quickly up the lonely

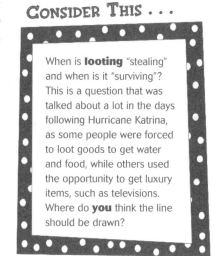

CONSIDER THIS . . .

When is **looting** "stealing" and when is it "surviving"? This is a question that was talked about a lot in the days following Hurricane Katrina, as some people were forced to loot goods to get water and food, while others used the opportunity to get luxury items, such as televisions. Where do **you** think the line should be drawn?

streets. My mother and I got everyone up, telling them to pack as quickly as they could so we could leave. My grand-father looked outside and told us that there were looters stealing from the other stores around us. Knowing that they might do the same to our store, we put all of the expensive goods into the vault and made our second attempt at fleeing New Orleans.

This time we were lucky, and we found a way out of the city, which was now a city of chaos. As we passed buildings on fire, we saw some people stealing from their neighbors who had already left. I recognized some of the faces as our everyday customers. It looked as though the world was in the hands of Hades.

In search of a shelter, we heard of one over the fuzzy radio. It was called the Lamar-Dixon shelter in Gonzales, and it was a long two-hour drive to get there. And once we arrived, we had to stand in line in the beating hot sun just to register.

As we stayed in the Lamar-Dixon shelter, the days turned into weeks. To my surprise, the shelter wasn't as bad as I thought it would be. We were lucky to have such nice people next to us. As the weeks passed, my mother desperately tried to find someone who could help us get back to Minnesota, where we had moved from three years ago and still had family, but no one replied.

Then three weeks later, a man called and said he could help us. I was overwhelmed by joy. I was so happy, I almost forgot my worries about my boyfriend and my family members who I missed terribly. I was happy to know that I was going back to Minnesota, but was upset at the same time because my mother didn't want to come along. When I asked her "Why?" she would simply say, "Because of the store."

Oh, how I *hated* that store. I didn't even like Louisiana for that matter—ever since I had moved to New Orleans, things had been crummy for me. But even so, I pleaded more, hoping to hear that she would come. But she didn't.

We soon had to say our good-byes. And even though I'm thankful to everyone who helped us, leaving was very hard for me. On top of that, my boyfriend crushed my heart, breaking up with me and finding himself a new girlfriend two days later. My beloved mother stayed behind as well, and I don't get to talk to her at all. But I'm hopeful that our family will become whole again soon.

When I came back to my old school in Minnesota, I was greeted by all of my friends. In some ways, every day in Minnesota feels like my birthday because everyone here who helped my family and me has brought so much joy to us. And even though today I still struggle with feelings of pain, terror and worrying, I also have feelings of hope. I know that we need to cherish life as it is and be thankful for what we have—tomorrow is not promised to us.

Gabrielle Phan, Age 14

EDITOR'S NOTE: *Gabrielle's mother recently gave birth to a baby boy, and even though she hasn't met him yet, Gabrielle is looking forward to spending Christmas with her mom and her new brother.*

OUTSIDE THE BOX

When disaster strikes, it's hard to feel like we can make a difference unless we're on the ground physically helping those in need, but it's just not so. The next time there is a natural disaster and you want to get involved, here are some ideas for stepping up to the plate:

- Organize a fundraiser—have a bake sale or an arts and crafts sale, or go around to local businesses and ask them to donate goods for a sale. All the proceeds can go to the relief effort.
- Collect things—ask bookstores, libraries and local authors to donate extra stock and send them to teens in the affected areas.
- Create a care package—put together a care package of the five things you couldn't live without, and send it to a teen who's been affected through the local YMCA or YWCA.
- Volunteer—Contact your local Red Cross and see if there are local relief efforts that you can get involved in.
- Think small—you don't have to donate thousands of dollars to have a big impact. Even if your effort only affects one person, the difference you'll make in his or her life will be immeasurable.

Take the Quiz:

ARE YOU PREPARED TO HANDLE LOSSES IN YOUR LIFE?

1. You know that dogs don't live as long as people do, but the thought of your aging beloved pet not being around for the rest of your life is difficult to come to grips with. You know that your pet is sick and doesn't have much time left. How do you handle it?

___ A. You are devastated about your pet's condition, but you know that you have to cherish the time you have left together. You do everything you can to comfort your pet and let him know how much he means to you. You're so sad, but you also know that your dog will be out of his discomfort soon.

___ B. It's hard to watch your pet getting older, and you distance yourself from him so you don't have to deal with all the pain you're feeling inside. You love him more than anything, but this is really hard to go through.

___ C. You are in complete denial about your pet's failing health and decide to ignore what's going on. If you don't think about it, there's nothing to worry about.

2. Your best friend's mom has just gotten a great promotion at work, but it means her family is relocating to another state. Worse yet, everything is happening so fast—your friend will be gone by the end of the month. What do you do?

___ A. You're sad that your best friend is moving, but you know that the move is probably going to be even harder on her. You focus your energy on comforting your friend and send her off with a care package and a plan for staying in close touch.

___ B. Your initial reaction is anger at your friend—how could she leave you behind like this? But after a few weeks, you snap out of it and try to squeeze in some quality time with her before it's too late.

___ C. You cannot fathom life in middle school without your best friend by your side. You fall into a deep funk and cry yourself to sleep every night, hoping you'll wake up to find this nightmare is over.

3. Your grandma has been sick for a long time now, and it doesn't look like she'll be getting better. She's just been transferred from the hospital to hospice care in your house so that you can all be together for her last months. You are extremely close with your grandmother and find the whole thing overwhelming. How do you cope?

___ A. You feel honored to be able to take care of your beloved grandma during her last days. You spend as much time as possible with her, making sure she knows just how much you love her.

___ B. You have a tough time handling your emotions so you keep them locked up inside and try to act like everything's going to be okay whenever you're around your grandma.

___ C. Seeing your grandma so sick is just too hard to take, so you try to spend as much time away from home as possible. You figure she's got enough people taking care of her that she won't miss your presence.

4. It's your first week of high school, and things just haven't turned out the way you imagined at all. Your boyfriend dumped you the week before school started, and your close-knit clique seems to have scattered to the four corners of the Earth. Nothing is turning out the way you thought it would be. What do you do?

___ A. You are disappointed that things aren't the way you expected, but you try to remain optimistic that things will get better. Maybe you'll even find a better boyfriend and friends!

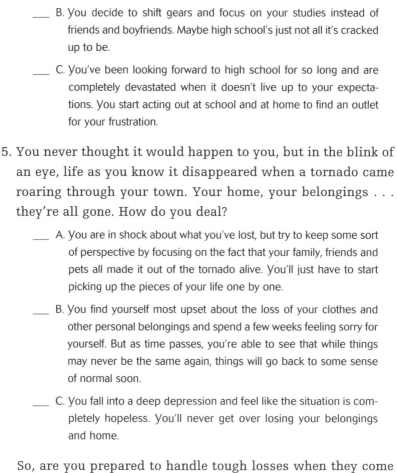

___ B. You decide to shift gears and focus on your studies instead of friends and boyfriends. Maybe high school's just not all it's cracked up to be.

___ C. You've been looking forward to high school for so long and are completely devastated when it doesn't live up to your expectations. You start acting out at school and at home to find an outlet for your frustration.

5. You never thought it would happen to you, but in the blink of an eye, life as you know it disappeared when a tornado came roaring through your town. Your home, your belongings . . . they're all gone. How do you deal?

___ A. You are in shock about what you've lost, but try to keep some sort of perspective by focusing on the fact that your family, friends and pets all made it out of the tornado alive. You'll just have to start picking up the pieces of your life one by one.

___ B. You find yourself most upset about the loss of your clothes and other personal belongings and spend a few weeks feeling sorry for yourself. But as time passes, you're able to see that while things may never be the same again, things will go back to some sense of normal soon.

___ C. You fall into a deep depression and feel like the situation is completely hopeless. You'll never get over losing your belongings and home.

So, are you prepared to handle tough losses when they come your way? Give yourself 10 points for every A, 20 points for every B and 30 points for every C:

50–70 points = While you can't possibly be expected to handle every difficult thing that comes your way perfectly, you definitely have a good approach when it comes to making sense of tragedy. You know that finding healthy ways to deal with your emotions and keeping things in perspective are the most important tools for dealing with loss.

80–120 points = Losses really throw you for a loop and are difficult to recover from, but eventually you find a way to get back up on your feet again. Try to use the lessons you learned from past losses to help you cope with those in the future.

130–150 points = You have great difficulty handling it when things don't go the way you'd hoped, especially involving serious losses. You might want to explore things like journal writing or other creative expression to find a way to let out pain that you're feeling.

STABBED IN THE BACK

eing stabbed in the back happens to everyone at some point in our life. Maybe a friend does something really insensitive or your boyfriend or girlfriend royally dumps you. Maybe some adult that you trusted did something that left you feeling like you didn't know what just hit you. Being stabbed in the back by someone doesn't have to be the end of the world, but it will force you to think about life and your relationships differently. This next chapter shares stories by teens who were stabbed in the back and are still here to write about it.

I FLIPPED ON THE *DR. PHIL* SHOW the other day and saw a story that totally blew my mind. This forty-year-old woman wanted to confront a girl from high school who she said used to tease and harass her in school. More than twenty years after the fact, this woman was still so angry at this former classmate that even talking about it on national television brought her to tears.

So Dr. Phil brought back the former bully so the woman could confront her and tell her how much pain her actions had caused over the years. While I found all of this rather interesting, what really got me was the fact that the former bully didn't even remember the other woman. She had no recollection of ever knowing her, let alone bullying and teasing her. And it wasn't just that she was in denial either. She clearly just didn't remember anything about it.

THE WORD

Selective memory is the idea that we remember things that are beneficial for us to remember, and forget the things that are too painful or don't further our cause.

Did this woman just have selective memory, or was it truly not a significant enough memory for it to stick with her over the past twenty-five years? Or did she really remember it, but was too ashamed to admit it on national television?

Whatever the answer, one thing is clear—the same event can be perceived and remembered by two people in completely different ways. It's our emotions and experiences that make all the difference. I'm sure if this former classmate knew that her actions in high school toward another girl would still be haunting her victim twenty-five years later, she would have made different choices. (At least I hope she would have.) That's the realization the author of this next story, "Joey's Pain," comes to on her own.

Joey's Pain

His name was Joseph Carta, but he became known to us as Joey. He had mental disabilities and was in a special class. A lot of people at our school made fun of him, and I want to confess that I laughed right along with the cruel remarks that were thrown at him every day.

A couple of months after he started at our school, we got shocking news: Joey had tried to kill himself by cutting his throat. But he didn't die—he missed his throat and cut his chin instead. He was ashamed when he came back to school, and he told us the reason for his absence was because of a trip to Disneyland.

CONSIDER THIS . . .

Even if you're not the one doing the **bullying**, by not taking a stand against it, the message you're sending is that it's okay.

"Then where did the stitches come from?" we taunted.

He told us he had tripped.

Read It?

Jerry Spinelli's novel *Crash* is written from the point of view of the bully, giving readers a chance to see what makes a bully tick.

We all laughed, and the teasing continued. A month later, Joey tried to shoot his little sister. Someone heard the shot and notified the police. The bullet had missed his sister, and Joey was taken away. I don't know whatever happened to him.

If I ever see Joey again, I want to tell him that I'm sorry. I'm sorry for all of the teasing, for all the pain he had to bear at our school. He had to deal with it all by himself, not a single friend to help him.

WHERE DO YOU STAND?

Have you been a bully and not realized it? Bullying takes on many different forms. Have you ever done any of the following?

___ **YES** Given someone you weren't
___ **NO**   getting along with the silent
           treatment?

___ **YES** Passed along a juicy tidbit of
___ **NO**   gossip that was circulating
           around the school?

___ **YES** Gotten other friends on your
___ **NO**   side and encouraged them to
           exclude someone else during
           a group fight?

___ **YES** Forwarded an e-mail that con-
___ **NO**   tained content meant to harass
           or make fun of someone else?

___ **YES** Stood by and did nothing while
___ **NO**   your friend or friends teased
           someone or called them
           names?

If you answered "yes" to even one of these questions, then you've been a bully.

You might think this is just a story of something that happened at our school. Maybe it is. But to me, it has a deeper meaning . . . love. The love that Joey never felt from us. If I could melt away time and return to the day when I first saw him, I would be Joey's friend. Someone he could share his thoughts, feelings and pain with. If you are reading this, please remember that everyone has feelings. Everyone has a heart. Are a few stupid comments worth hurting someone, causing them so much pain that they want to end it all? Please don't hurt other people . . . it's more worthwhile to love them.

Maggie Jo Kundla,
Age 13

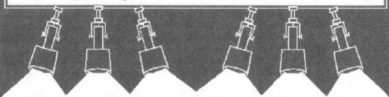

Spotlight On ... BULLYING

How do you define bullying? The definition is broader than you might think. Bullying doesn't just refer to kids beating up on other kids; it can be anything from exclusion and intimidation to name-calling and spreading gossip and rumors. And bullying is rampant in today's schools. In fact, 15% of all students are bullied on a regular basis. Most of these students are victims of verbal bullying as opposed to physical.

As technology has advanced, so have the strategies of bullies. "Cyber bullying," where kids IM and e-mail other kids with taunting words and threats, is becoming a real problem.

If you or a friend has ever been the target of bullying, you know that it's hard to know what to do when you're in that situation. You don't want to just take it without standing up for yourself, but you don't want to escalate the situation either. Here are some strategies for combating bullying when it gets personal:

- Avoid confrontation with the bully or bullies in the first place if you can. Stay close to friends, and if

possible, have a parent or friend pick you up after
school.

• Although you'll be tempted, don't retaliate, either
physically or verbally. Retaliation generally just
results in a worse situation.

• If the bullying is threatening or physical, tell an
adult—a parent, teacher, coach or guidance
counselor.

For more information, check out the Bullying Web
site at *www.bullying.org.*

HAVE YOU EVER HEARD OF THE TERM "GROUP MENTALITY"?
It's actually a real dynamic in psychology. It means that people in a
group do and say things that they wouldn't necessarily do if they
were alone. Being in a group can give people courage or a false
sense of security . . . even make them feel invincible. That's why
riots can happen when too many people rally around a controversial
cause. There's power in numbers, and unfortu-
nately even when that power is exhibited
in negative ways, we can still easily
get swept up in it.

The same thing can happen with
cliques in school. Even if some aspect of
the clique's behavior doesn't feel right, or
it doesn't represent the kind of person
you really are inside, it can be hard to

For Real?

Group mentality is
responsible for some
terrible events in history,
including the Salem
Witch Trials of 1692.

turn away from. Sometimes the comfort we feel in being part of a group overshadows those aspects that aren't so attractive to us. But what is the price we ultimately pay?

Memoirs of a Ganger

I recently decided to clean out my closet. It's a walk-in closet, but you wouldn't have known it from all of the stuff that had built up over the years. There wasn't even any room to move around. As I looked through the boxes, I came across one filled with piles of photos secured together by different colored rubber bands. The first photo I saw was one of me and my friends standing in a dressing room at Macy's. We were fourteen, and my friends wanted to try on prom dresses. I thought it was dumb. So, there we were—eight girls

Read It?

Clear Your Clutter with Feng Shui (pronounced *fung shway*) by Karen Kingston is a great book for helping you clean out both physical and emotional clutter you've got lying around so you don't become a pack rat.

in floor-length gowns, and on the far right, me, looking awkward, wearing a white peasant shirt with shiny metal braces on my teeth. To me, that picture represents how I always felt with my friends—comfortable, but oddly misplaced at the same time.

By the time I started high school, we had formed a clique. I wish I could say that even though I was in a clique that I remained kind to and respectful of my peers. This, however,

THE WORD

The word **scapegoat**, which means someone who gets the blame for what others do, comes from the words "escape" and "goat," and was translated from the Bible in the 1500s.

was not the case. For some reason, my clique always needed a scapegoat. Freshman and sophomore year, that scapegoat was Jesse. Jesse was friends with one of the girls in my clique, Sadie. But she didn't realize that as far as Sadie was concerned, their relationship was over as soon as high school began. So Jesse would follow us around, trying to be friendly and chatty. No one responded to her. Essentially, we just ignored her. Eventually, she got the message, but not until three of the girls in the group saw her coming toward them and hid in the bathroom atop the toilets. Jesse may have been some things, but she wasn't stupid. She didn't try to talk to us after the bathroom incident.

We were mean to other girls, too. However, perhaps worst of all, we talked about each other behind our own backs. This past summer, all of us except two of the girls were helping another pack for a trip. One of the two missing girls called, and when the girl whose house we were at shut off the phone, she and three others proceeded to talk badly about the friend who had called. The rest of us just sat there and said nothing. But as it turns out, the phone hadn't shut off properly, and our friend heard the whole

HOW ABOUT YOU?

Have you ever **not** spoken up because you were trying to **avoid** hurting someone's feelings?

conversation about her. Then we heard her voice come through the phone.

"The next time you're going to talk about me, make sure to shut off your phone first," she said.

Absolute silence.

The worst part of that whole experience was that the friend on the phone wasn't upset with me because I hadn't actually said anything bad about her. It made me think of a quote from a fifth-grade textbook. We were studying racial segregation in the school systems of the 1960s. The quote read: "To throw bricks is bad, but to stand and watch the bricks being thrown and not do anything is even worse." The same way bystanders watched as others were physically abused, I had watched and listened as my friend was verbally abused. I felt that I had failed my friend.

It's now the end of senior year, and I'm happy to say that while the clique still exists, it is and has been diminishing rapidly since the events of last year. While it would be nice to claim the group is practically gone because we all realized how immature it was, in reality we simply grew apart. Although I will see all of my friends at the beginning of this summer, I know I will not speak to over half of them next year in college. The clique was a large part of my high-school experience, but something I must say good-bye to, along with the person I was. Backstabbing and double-crossing are

For Real?

It was only a little more than 40 years ago that the **Civil Rights Movement** made racial segregation in schools illegal, in large part thanks to civil rights activists like Rosa Parks and Martin Luther King, Jr.

actions I intend to leave behind me and not carry over to college. Unbelievably, it really is almost over. Good-bye, gang.

Terry Beasley, Age 18

Are you hanging out with a backstabbing friend? Here's how to make a clean break:

- Talk to your friend about what's going on and give him or her the benefit of the doubt before taking action.
- Figure out what you want to say before you say it so you don't lose your cool or get anxious when you have your pow wow.
- Decide what you want the outcome of the talk to be before you begin. If you want to try and work things out, let him or her know that up front.
- Try not to get angry and say things that you might regret later.
- If a face-to-face conversation is too scary, try getting your thoughts out in a letter or e-mail.
- Follow your gut. If something inside is telling you that this friendship just isn't healthy, then maybe it's time to get out.

IF YOU'VE EVER TRULY BEEN STABBED IN THE BACK by a friend, you know that sometimes the hurt can be as bad as if a real blade had been used. And it can throw you for a real loop—making you question everything that had ever happened in the friendship. Was it all just a lie? Can you ever trust anyone again?

It might be hard to do, but it's almost always worth it to trust again. Just because one or two people screwed you over doesn't mean that no one else deserves a chance to get close. But at the same time, you can protect yourself by being smart about your trust. Sometimes trust needs to be earned, and if you follow your gut and pay attention to warning signs that things might not be heading in the right direction, then hopefully you won't find yourself stabbed in the back anymore.

Read It?

Being Bindy by Alyssa Brugman features Janie, who is hung out to dry by her best friend.

Hung Out to Dry

I met my best friend, Sarah, when I was in seventh grade. At first, we had our ups and downs like most new friendships, but then we grew close, and she became the kind of best friend any girl would love to have.

When we were in eighth grade, Sarah's dad died from diabetes, and she was devastated. And after that, Sarah started to change into someone else. That someone else wasn't the best friend I used to have—she had become a rebellious teenager.

The summer before we were to start high school, Sarah met someone named K.C. I knew that K.C. was everything I didn't

Seen It?

Thirteen (2003) is a powerful movie about a girl who got sucked into trouble by hanging out with the wrong friend.

want in a friend, but I stuck with them both until we had become an inseparable trio. That summer, we hung out just about every day.

Since I was always with my two friends, I wasn't at home or with my family very much, and they started to get worried about me. I think that my two best friends weren't the kind of friends they had hoped I'd find.

One weekend during freshman year, my friendship with K.C. and Sarah took a major U-turn. The three of us had walked to the mall together, with Sarah's boyfriend tagging along. I had a few dollars with me that my parents had given me for food and something small. We ended up in Macy's, and that's when things got weird. K.C. handed me a few ring sets and some bracelets and said, "Hold these. I got a little surprise for you and Sarah." Little did I know that she had five-finger discounted them. Without thinking, I put all of them in my pocket. When we walked out of the store, three security guards came out of nowhere yelling, "Stop! Stop!"

I froze in shock and turned around. The guards said that they saw someone stealing jewelry on their security tapes. At that moment my heart was beating a million times a second. Everything was going through my head at once.

For Real?

About one-quarter of all **shoplifters** are between the ages of 14 and 17. Even though most teens start shoplifting because of boredom or depression, it can become an **addiction** quickly.

How could my friends do this to me? I thought. If that wasn't bad enough, the security guards pulled the merchandise out of my pocket, and I was stuck with the blame. My two "best friends" didn't even say a word to help me out. They left the store in the clear. I was speechless. Security took me into a little room with handcuffs attached to benches, made note of my information and took my picture. Then they called my parents. My mom came and picked me up. When she first got the call about her daughter stealing, she said she thought it was a prank.

CONSIDER THIS . . .

> Even though **shoplifting** might not seem like a big deal, the **consequences** can be pretty **serious**. Teens who are arrested for shoplifting might have a permanent criminal record, which will affect job applications, college admissions, and much more.

When we went outside, my mom started screaming at me, asking me what I was thinking. So, I told her what happened. She decided that I wasn't allowed to see my friends again.

Since then, I haven't talked to my friends. I've seen them around school, but I'm too ashamed to talk to them. When they did try to apologize, I was too upset to accept it. That was the day my best friends betrayed me. I still think about those days spent with Sarah and K.C. and how it would be today if we were all still friends—I wouldn't be able to ignore what a bad influence she was on me any longer. And as I move forward, I've learned to pay attention to warning signs when it comes my friends, and remember that if I don't feel comfortable being who I am with my friends, it's not worth it.

Lindsey Walker, Age 18

OUTSIDE THE BOX

Do you have a friend who treats you badly, makes you feel not-so-good about yourself, and just isn't cutting it when it comes to what best friends are supposed to be all about? Here are three steps for handling the situation:

1. Get perspective. Talk with a parent or older brother or sister to find out if what's going on is typical friendship behavior.

2. Don't stick with a friend just because you're afraid of not having someone to hang out with. When you make room by getting rid of a negative friendship, a healthy one can come in and replace it.

3. Talk to the friend and see if they're willing to deal with your concerns. If they're not, it's time to move on!

WHERE DO YOU STAND?

Do you put up with too much stuff from your friends?

Your BFF seems to take pleasure in pointing out your little flaws in front of other people just to get a laugh. Do you let it slide?

- NO, NOT ME (0 points)
- DEPENDS ON THE SITUATION (1 point)
- YEAH, PROBABLY (2 points)

Your friend makes plans that include you without checking with you first. He's always assuming you'll be up for whatever he suggests. Do you go along with it, no questions asked?

- NO, NOT ME (0 points)
- DEPENDS ON THE SITUATION (1 point)
- YEAH, PROBABLY (2 points)

Your S.O. blew you off at the homecoming dance and then the next day acted like everything was fine. Do you keep your mouth shut about the dance?

- NO, NOT ME (0 points)
- DEPENDS ON THE SITUATION (1 point)
- YEAH, PROBABLY (2 points)

Your friend asked for your help designing a program for the upcoming soccer tournament she's organizing. You end up doing all the work, but she gladly takes all the credit. Do let her bask in all the glory?

- NO, NOT ME (0 points)
- DEPENDS ON THE SITUATION (1 point)
- YEAH, PROBABLY (2 points)

You came up behind your group of friends in the hallway only to catch an earful of dirt your friend was scooping about you to everyone else. Do you pretend you didn't hear so as not to make any waves?

- NO, NOT ME (0 points)
- DEPENDS ON THE SITUATION (1 point)
- YEAH, PROBABLY (2 points)

Add up your points:

    0–3 = You don't let anyone push you around.

    4–7 = You weigh each situation carefully before acting.

    8–10 = You need to stand up for yourself more.

YEARS AGO, I HAD A CLOSE FRIEND NAMED LAURIE.
Laurie had this huge crush on a new guy, Ben, who went to school
with us. She and Ben became good friends, and as they started
hanging out together, I would tag along because Laurie and I were
always together. As the weeks wore on, it became clear that while
Laurie still had a crush on Ben, he didn't like her "that way." He
treated her more like a sister or friend.

This was all just fine, until one night when Ben told me that I
was the one he liked. Even as I write this, I'm still filled with guilt that
I didn't turn away from his advances. Within a matter of days, Ben
and I were boyfriend and girlfriend. Laurie was livid with me—with
the whole situation. I couldn't blame her either, but I had gotten so
caught up in the romance with Ben that I chose to accept her
anger and did nothing to make things right.

When Ben and I broke up a few months later and I realized that
he wasn't even close to being worth losing my friend over, I tried
my best to make things right with Laurie. Over time, she forgave
me, and we got back some of the closeness we once had. I'm so
thankful that she gave me another chance. I hope that I would
have done the same if I were in her shoes, just like the author of
this next story, "Forgiving the Unforgivable".

Forgiving the Unforgivable

I remember the first time I ever laid eyes upon Alison. I was in first grade and the new kid in school. We were out on the playground for recess, and I was playing hopscotch with a couple of new friends. I looked up and saw a group of girls gathered around a pretty little blonde with long earrings. I was instantly convinced she had to be someone special to have so many admirers, and from that day on, I knew I had to be her friend.

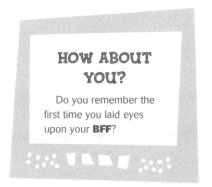

HOW ABOUT YOU?

Do you remember the first time you laid eyes upon your **BFF**?

In time, we became the best of friends. I loved spending time at her house. She had the coolest toys to play with and a huge backyard to explore. The older we got, the closer we became. We had our own special little group of friends, and we remained close all through grade school.

Sometime between middle school and high school, Alison and I lost touch with each other. She became interested in horses and met other friends, while I remained a social butterfly, interested in boys and partying. Junior year came, and Alison and I found each other in a couple of the same

CONSIDER THIS . . .

When a **friend** goes through **changes**, it can be challenging to make things work. But if you both want to keep the friendship alive, it can be done. And just think—if it's something you're **both** willing to work hard at, your friendship might end up being even stronger than before.

classes. As soon as we started talking, the old bond instantly rekindled as though it had been there the entire time. We started spending more time together, and pretty soon became inseparable once again. It was Alison who I turned to when I had a fight with my parents, when school got too hard, and when I lost one of my best friends. She was also the one I turned to when I had my first broken heart. I can recall countless nights spent crying my eyes out to her over this guy who had meant the world to me. She was the only one who seemed to really understand what I was going through, and she stuck by my side the entire time.

Alison never complained about how much I cried . . . she just sat there patiently and listened to me rant on and on about him. She would kindly tell me that I could do better, that he didn't deserve me, and that I would find my Prince Charming soon enough. Alison was helping me get over my heartbreak. She was more than my best friend—she was a sister to me, and I trusted her with my life. Until one night over Christmas break changed everything.

For Real?

The name "Prince Charming" was first used in Walt Disney's animated movie *Cinderella* (1950), and since then, the princes in other Disney movies such as *Snow White and the Seven Dwarfs* and *Sleeping Beauty* have also been given this name.

It had been a rough couple of months for me, and I was having a bad night. I was on the computer talking to Alison. She could always make me feel better about anything, until now. I still remember how it felt when she told me she had hooked-up with the same guy who had broken my heart, the same one who I was still hurting over. My whole body went numb. I couldn't move. I couldn't speak. I just stared at the computer screen in complete shock, thinking, *She must be joking. She would never do this to me. Not Alison, not my best friend, not the one I had cried countless times to about this guy.*

I didn't know what to say. My mind was bombarded with a ton of emotions—anger, confusion, pain. I felt like someone had taken a dagger and shoved it straight into my heart. My trust was shattered. I sat in my room and cried to a mutual friend for hours. I knew Alison was sorry, and I knew I didn't want to lose her as a friend, but how could I forgive her? I just couldn't understand *why* she did it.

> ## CONSIDER THIS . . .
>
> **Holding on** to **anger** over something that has already happened is a choice you make every day. Make the choice to **let go** of the anger, and the feelings that go with it will disappear, too.

I didn't speak to Alison for a couple of weeks. I needed time to think, to absorb it all. But I gave it a lot of thought, and after much deliberation, I decided to forgive her. No one is perfect; we all make mistakes. I knew Alison meant it when she said she was sorry, and I didn't think this guy was worth losing my best friend over. I had already lost so much; I just couldn't stand losing her. Though it wasn't easy to pick up where we left off, we started slowly. The more time we spent together, the more my trust in her was restored. I knew if I held on to that anger, I would only be hurting myself. God says to forgive others as you would want him to be forgiven, and that's just what I did.

Andi Parker, Age 18

OUTSIDE THE BOX

If you've been betrayed by a friend and want to move on, here are some ways to deal:

- Take time to gather your thoughts before taking action.
- Figure out if you need to take any of the blame for what happened.
- Tell your friend how you feel and give them a chance to apologize.
- When you're ready, let go of the anger.

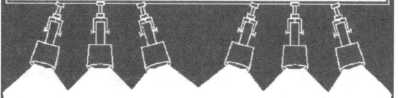

Spotlight On . . . WHEN FRIENDS CHANGE

Have you ever had a friend who's changed right before your eyes? Or maybe you've been the one to change, and the things that you used to have in common with your BFF just don't appeal to you anymore. Well, that's completely normal. In fact, *change* is normal. Just look around you. Things change every minute of every day—our hair grows longer, our mood shifts, the grass grows. And while sometimes there are big events that spur on a change in someone, like trouble at home or a new boyfriend or girlfriend, other times it's as simple as one friend exploring a new interest and the other friend choosing not to.

So is change always bad? Definitely not. But it can be challenging to get through, especially if your friend's behavior is changing and you can't figure out why. If you've got a friend who has changed, here are some ideas for coming to terms with it, and maybe even salvaging your friendship:

- Remember that change is part of life. Think positively and try to see the positive side of the change, if there is one.
- If your friend is changing in ways that concern you, talk with them about how you feel. On the other hand, if your friend is simply exploring new interests, give them the room to do this without them worrying if you'll still be there for them.

WHEN SOMEONE THAT YOU ARE REALLY INTO TELLS YOU that they "just want to be friends" or that they "just don't feel the same way" about you as you feel about them, it can be really hard to take. How can we not take it personally? After all, it is a rejection, right? They are saying they don't like us. Even if it's not right, sometimes anger is the only emotion that comes out. That's the sentiment of the next author's poem, "You to Blame."

You to Blame

What does, "I'm not ready for a relationship" mean?
It plays like the record in a broken dream.
It was more like a nightmare to hear you say
"I'm not feeling for you the same way."
I feel my heart crumble as there is emptiness inside,
There's nowhere to go, no place to hide.
I miss you more with every day,
Why can't you understand the words I say?
I feel alone, and sadness, too
All I wanted was to be with you.
Now I'm left with all this pain,
And I only have you to blame.

Kaylee Starr, Age 18

HOW ABOUT YOU?

Have you ever heard the words **"I just don't feel the same way as you do"?** How did you feel when you heard them?

CONSIDER THIS . . .

Being dumped doesn't have to be looked at like a bad rejection. If we were perfect for everyone, the dating scene would be pretty difficult to navigate. Instead, think of being dumped as an opportunity to find someone you're *really* compatible with!

Seen It?

In the movie *Cruel Intentions* (1999), Reese Witherspoon's character is pressured into having sex, even though she had planned to wait until she was married.

WHEN YOU'RE IN A SERIOUS RELATIONSHIP WITH SOMEONE, there's nothing worse than having your trust shattered by the person you shared your heart with. If the relationship was really intense and sex was involved, the betrayal can bring on all kinds of complex feelings. Many teens today are choosing to abstain from sex for this very reason. Because the reality is, when sex becomes a part of a relationship, the stakes are much higher. The emotions are more intense, and the potential for pain is much greater—for girls and boys alike.

Thunder Still Roars

We had something special, something neither of us had ever felt before. We called each other every day to plan our nights out together. I loved how he treated me. I wanted so badly to carve "Madison loves Taylor" in a big oak tree. I was the one he cared most about. I was his angel.

We did the typical high-school things when we hung out—watched a movie at home or went out to a party and socialized. We acted just like a married couple. In fact, that was how our friends viewed us, since we were always together having such a great time.

It rained a lot over the summer, so we would get together at his house and watch movies all night long. It was great because we loved spending time together, being by each other's side.

As was often the case, one night his parents weren't home—they were caught up in traffic on sleek streets after a full day of furniture shopping. His parents trusted us and knew that we loved each other enough not to try something sneaky.

HOW ABOUT YOU?

Do your parents ever leave you **alone** with your boyfriend or girlfriend at home?

The movie had just ended. Taylor set off into his room and closed the door behind him. I wasn't sure if I was supposed to follow him or just sit on the couch waiting for him to come back. Feeling awkward sitting there, I eventually followed him into his room to see if everything was okay.

"Hon, are you alright?" I asked.

"Yeah, I'm fine, just a little tired."

Taylor lay down in his bed, so I laid down right next to him and curled up in his arms. Out of nowhere, a question popped out of my mouth.

"Taylor, will you marry me?"

He gave a quiet chuckle and responded with, "Sure babe."

Suddenly, I was the happiest I'd

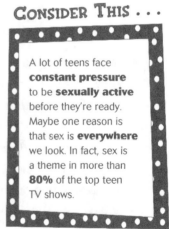

CONSIDER THIS . . .

A lot of teens face **constant pressure** to be **sexually active** before they're ready. Maybe one reason is that sex is **everywhere** we look. In fact, sex is a theme in more than **80%** of the top teen TV shows.

ever been. He said he would marry me! This was the boy I didn't think I could live without, much less get through my last year of high school while he was off in his first year of college. Happily, I kissed his lips about twenty times.

"Dang, that's a whole lot of kisses," he said quietly.

"Well, I just want to show you how much I love you," I added.

For Real?

The average age of a man in the U.S. when he gets **married** is 26 years old. For women, it's 25.

It started thundering and lightning outside, and shortly after the power went out. It was almost pitch black in the house. I was scared of the dark, but since he was with me and would never let anything happen to me, I felt just fine.

Then, suddenly, I felt that he expected more from me than just kisses.

"What are you doing?" I asked him in shock.

"I just want to show you how much I love you, babe."

I couldn't believe what was happening. This was the boyfriend who wouldn't try anything unless he got the okay from me. Why hadn't he asked? He knew I would say no. Why was he forcing this?

Unsure, I let Taylor show his love to me. Looking back, I realized in that moment I felt confident that I was going to spend the rest of my life with Taylor, now, I think I didn't want him to assume I didn't like him by stopping him. I knew he wouldn't leave me after this—he always told me how much he loved me and meant it.

For Real?

Nearly **40%** of teens say that **relationship issues** are one of their biggest concerns.

Midnight came, and I had to go home. I lived in the same neighborhood, but like the sweet guy he is,

Taylor offered to take me home because that was more time we could spend together. I couldn't wait to get in my room and leap on my bed. At home, I waited for him to call me like he always did, but that night, I never heard his ring. I wondered if he had gotten home okay. I called him as soon as that thought popped into my mind. He answered with an annoyed tone in his voice. He asked if he could call me back tomorrow.

Tomorrow came. Why hadn't he woken me up with a call in the morning? He was usually my human alarm clock, always there to welcome in a new day.

Later that afternoon, I finally called him. He asked me to come over to his house. I bolted up to my room, got my shoes and ran over to his house. I usually never had to ring his doorbell—he was always waiting outside for me. Except that day, he wasn't. *Maybe he's busy,* I thought. I went in, hurrying so I could hug him and be in his arms.

"Hi, sweetie!" I shouted as I entered his room.

Taylor was sitting on his bed with a weird look on his face. He looked really serious.

"What's wrong?" I asked in deep concern.

The words that came out of his mouth were the last ones I expected.

"I don't think we should be together."

What was wrong? We were so happy! He couldn't leave me . . . I wouldn't make it. Why was he doing this to me? I burst into tears and stared at him with hatred, while the thunder roared outside. Then he told me that he wasn't in love with me anymore. I couldn't believe my ears. How could I have been so stupid and not stopped him yesterday? I wanted to run home and cry forever.

"Do you want to go home?" he asked me quietly.

"Yeah," I said with a stutter.

We walked downstairs with unspoken words. He opened the door for me, and I headed out toward his truck. Grabbing the handle, I looked up and found he wasn't even there anymore. I set off onto my long journey home alone, my clothes drenched with rain and mud all over my shoes, while lightning lit up the sky.

The biggest regret of my life happened the night before. If I had just said "No," maybe we'd still be together or curled up watching movies somewhere. My trust in Taylor has been ruined forever. Getting hurt was the last thing I wanted from him. That night of the roaring thunder has changed my life forever. It was the night all girls should think about before they do anything. You may not think about it at first, but thunder still roars.

Madison, Age 15

OUTSIDE THE BOX

If you're concerned about facing sexual pressure, here are some strategies for sticking with your plan:

- Avoid situations where you might feel pressure to have sex in the first place.
- Don't drink or do drugs—they impair your judgment.
- Learn how to say "no" and mean it.
- Remember that if the person really loves you, they'll respect your feelings (I know this sounds cliché, but it's true!).
- Take a course in self-defense.
- Be prepared and have a plan for how you'll handle a pressure-filled situation before you're in it.

THERE'S SOMETHING ESPECIALLY STINGING ABOUT BEING humiliated by a teacher. The whole thing is so . . . *so public.* Teachers have so much authority at school, so much respect, that when they do or say something about us that isn't fair, unfortunately it can still carry a lot of weight.

The author of this next essay, "Standing Short," found it within herself to take public humiliation by a teacher and learn an important lesson about acceptance. Now if only some teachers could learn the same lesson . . .

Standing Short

Looking back, I guess I should have known it was coming. The thing is, I never would have thought she would say anything like that. She was a teacher. She wasn't supposed to criticize my appearance.

I was in tenth grade when I decided to try out for my school's annual musical production. Because my school was so small, most people who audition get parts, so it really wasn't supposed to be a big deal. You just get up and read a few lines. To me, though, it turned out to be an experience that I'm not likely to soon forget.

When I was called up to read lines for the first time, it was for a small, non-singing part. Though I was hoping for something a little bigger, I read the script with as much feeling as I could muster and returned to my seat. Later, after some of my schoolmates read for parts too, I was called up again to read the part of the lead.

I didn't know what to think. There were other students who

hadn't auditioned for anything yet, and I wondered if the teacher had forgotten that I'd already read. Yet, other teachers were there too, so I figured they would notice if it was a mistake. Despite my ponderings and the fact that I wasn't particularly interested in such a large role, I got up and took the script.

For Real?

In the mid 1800s, the average American man was just over 5'7" tall, while today the average is 5'9". Scientists attribute the growth to better health and nutrition.

It so happened that the boy picked to read the part opposite me stood at an amazing six feet, five inches tall. Next to him, anyone appears to be short, but as I'm an even five feet tall, the difference was more than awkward.

Since I knew everyone was already thinking about how unsuited our heights were, I laughed and teased, "Oh, this is perfect!"

HOW ABOUT YOU?

Have you ever been **humiliated** by a teacher? How did you handle it?

The next thing I knew, one of the teachers exclaimed, "No! Allyssa can't be the oldest daughter! She's *too short!*"

I was shocked and embarrassed beyond belief. I'd been teased by my friends about my stature before, but I hadn't ever minded; they'd just been joking. My teacher wasn't. There I was, in front of about fifteen of my peers, being told flat-out that I couldn't even audition for a part because of my height. Numbly, I returned to my seat and watched as another girl read the lines instead. She was taller than me.

I felt so discriminated against that I didn't let the incident go. I told my parents all about it, as well as other teachers, and the next day my drama teacher pulled me out of a class to make sure I was all right.

When the parts for the musical were announced, I received the small, non-singing part in which I was supposed to be nine years old. At the time, I felt the only reason I had received any part at all was because I'd made such a huge deal about the comment made about me. Even if that was the case, I've participated in other drama productions since then and have been cast in better roles, so my ability to participate in school productions hasn't suffered as a result of my short stature after all.

Since this incident, I've realized that discrimination in any form is wrong. Even though I've gotten over the fact that I am, and probably will always be, five feet tall, what I learned at that audition is that it matters how I treat people, and others can be affected by the things I say. People shouldn't judge others by the way they look. What really matters is *who you are*, not how tall you might be, what clothes you wear, or what you look like. It turned out that these are lessons even some adults still need to learn. I'm glad that I learned them now while I'm still young.

Allyssa Gleason, Age 17

> ## CONSIDER THIS . . .
>
> **Short stature** doesn't have any effect on the appeal of these **stars**:
> - Reese Witherspoon –5'2"
> - Kylie Minogue–5'1"
> - Rose McGowan–5'1"
> - Tom Cruise–5'7"

Seen It?

The movie *Simon Birch* (1998) is about a short boy who feels his height—or lack of it—is a gift from God.

OUTSIDE THE BOX

You probably know what an audition's all about from watching <u>American Idol</u>, but here are some tips for having your best audition:

- Get a good night's sleep the night before so you're on top of your game.
- Do relaxation exercises, like deep breathing, to calm your nerves.
- Take the time to warm up your voice or your body, depending on what you're auditioning for.
- Read up on the play and part that you're auditioning for.
- Wear something comfortable that you feel confident in.

Take the Quiz:
CAN YOU HANDLE BEING STABBED IN THE BACK

1. It's finals week at school, and you've been studying your butt off, so you're more than annoyed when your friend keeps trying to sneak a peek at your science test to get your answers. Things go from bad to worse when the teacher asks you both to stay after class and busts you both for cheating. Your friend doesn't take all the blame. What do you do?

   ___ A. You are mad at your friend, but don't want to risk alienating her and the rest of your friends by telling the truth and clearing your name. You're afraid everyone would think you're a tattletale and stop wanting to be your friend, so you just suck it up and suffer the consequences.

   ___ B. You're really annoyed with your friend, but don't want to make a big deal out of it. You convince your teacher to give you another chance and let you take an essay test after school to prove you know your stuff.

   ___ C. You talk with the teacher after school and explain what happened. Then you tell your friend that if she wants to make things right with you, she's got to tell the teacher the truth and 'fess up.

2. Your best friend has always acted like you're number one, but when a new cool girl starts at your school, things start to change. Suddenly, your BFF is treating you like a second-class citizen, and you feel like you're being seriously taken for granted. How do you handle it?

   ___ A. You decide to go out of your way to prove to your best friend why you're so important to her, and take every opportunity to try and make the new girl look bad.

___ B. You don't like being squeezed out, so you do what you can to stay in the loop, including befriending the new girl yourself. Who knows? Maybe the three of you will become inseparable.

___ C. You are hurt by your friend's actions, and you decide to tell your friend how she's making you feel. If things don't change after a heart-to-heart, maybe it's time to find a new best friend.

3. You've had a flirtatious relationship with a girl in your Spanish class all year, and all of your friends know about your crush on her. So you can't believe your eyes when you spot one of your closest friends making out with her under the bleachers after a basketball game. What's your next step?

___ A. You feel beyond betrayed and wait for your friend outside the school. When he comes out to go home, you get in his face and read him the riot act—how could he go after a girl you liked?

___ B. You are upset, but don't want to let any of your friends know how much this hurt. You shrug it off with a laugh, but decide to keep your crushes to yourself from now on.

___ C. You call your friend on it the next time you see him and let him know that he's lost your trust. If he wants to stay friends with you, he'd better explain what happened and do what he can to make things right.

4. It seems that no matter what you get involved in at school, your best friend follows suit. What's worse, she tries to compete with you at every turn. You don't really want to be in competition with your best friend, but she seems to be forcing the situation, even trying to sabotage your efforts to make herself look better. How do you cope?

___ A. Your friend picked the wrong person to compete with—her efforts only make you try harder to top her in every activity. Besides, if she can play dirty, so can you.

___ B. You think it's kind of lame that your friend is competing with you so much and stopping at nothing to win. You decide to drop out of some of the activities and let her have her moment of glory. It's not worth losing a friendship over.

___ C. You realize that it's only natural for you both to be interested in the same things. That's probably one reason why you're friends in the first place. You focus on doing your own thing as best you can without making it personal.

5. You're going through some pretty painful and very personal problems in your home life, and you've shared every last detail with your best friend in the closest of confidence. You are speechless when another friend lets something slip, and you realize that your secrets weren't actually being kept safe after all. How do you handle it?

___ A. You are livid when you discover your best friend has been spilling the beans, and you let her know it. As soon as you're done telling her how you feel, you dump her as a friend.

___ B. You feel betrayed by your friend, but you don't want to make waves so you don't say anything about it. You give her the benefit of the doubt and assume that she is generally trustworthy.

___ C. You confront your friend and give her a chance to explain and then let her know that she's lost your trust. You don't want to lose her friendship, but you won't be confiding in her anymore.

So, do you know how to handle getting stabbed in the back? Give yourself 10 points for every A, 20 points for every B, and 30 points for every C:

50–70 points = While friends might disappoint you from time to time, you don't do or say anything to let them know that the way they're acting toward you is not okay. We teach people how to treat us, so spend a little time teaching your friends that there are some things that they just can't do if they want to remain your friend.

80–120 points = You take each situation as it comes and try to figure out a solution that involves as little confrontation as possible. Try speaking up for yourself a little more—you might find you get great results.

130–150 points = You have high expectations in your friendships, and you let people know when they've let you down. If someone doesn't treat you with the respect that you deserve as a friend, you're not afraid to let them know it, but you usually give them a chance to make the situation right.

CHAPTER 6

WHAT'S HAPPENING OUT THERE?

While we can have some degree of control in our lives when it comes to the friends we choose, the choices we make and the clothes we wear, when it comes to what's happening in our community or our city or our world, for the most part, it's out of our hands. We are left to our own devices to find a way to make sense of the events that happen, whether across the ocean or in our own backyard. In this chapter, teens reflect on events in the outside world that have shaped who they are and share some ideas for making sense of it all.

AS A WRITER WHO WORKS WITH TEENS, adults ask me all the time what issues today's teens are dealing with. One question they always ask is: "Is teenhood and adolescence more difficult for today's teens than when we were teenagers?"

I always start my answer the same way. I say, "yes and no." Yes, I say, many of the things today's teens struggle with are the same things we all faced at one time—peer pressure, sexual pressure, self-image problems, a need to fit in, academic pressure, coming from broken homes, and so on. But then I explain the "no" part of my answer. And I tell people that while the problems in many ways might appear to be the same, the world today is a much different place than it was ten, twenty, thirty years ago. And that changes everything.

The last ten years have seen some of the most devastating tragedies in U.S. history, topped off, of course, with 9/11 and including things like the Columbine school shooting and the increased awareness of terrorist threats. There is so much fear surrounding our everyday lives that sometimes it takes all of our energy to prevent that fear from seeping into everything we do.

This next powerful essay, "Living in a World of Fear," is a bold statement by a teen who has decided to take a stand and not give in to the culture of violence that was thrust upon her small community.

Living in a World of Fear

I am absent-mindedly jingling my keys while waiting in line at the grocery store when the girl in front of me buying a frozen pizza strikes up a conversation.

She asks me what high school I go to.

"Basha High School," is my reply.

"Oooh," she says, a look of realization dawning on her. "That's where the crazy girl used to go."

"No," I correct her, doing my best to hold back a flood of anger. "That's where *Kelley* used to go."

It has been almost four months since high-school junior Kelly Kaminski was arrested on multiple counts of interfering with an educational institution. While the story of a planned school shooting may not be front-page news anymore, it definitely hasn't stopped impacting the lives of all who knew her.

For Real?

In 1998, more than 3,500 students in the U.S. were **expelled** for carrying **guns** to school. More than **40%** of them were in elementary or middle school.

In April 2005, other BHS students heard Kelley talking to two of her friends in the lunchroom about plans they had made for a school shooting. An investigation was conducted, and police found a notebook containing detailed plans and a diagram. When a search warrant was obtained for her house, it was confirmed that Kelley had access to assault rifles, handguns and ammunition. (They were her stepdad's).

To say our school was in a state of panic would be an understatement. Safety measures were tightened for a few weeks, with extra security guards sent over from

Address Book

Most states and cities have anonymous tip-lines to call in with any concerns about **violence** at your **school**. To find one near you, do a Google search under the terms: "school violence tipline" + your state or city.

neighboring high schools. A meeting was held for concerned parents, and our principal was there to professionally answer their questions. Cameras and the media were omnipresent during the next few days. Suddenly, everyone knew about our high school.

What was of prime concern to many of us as students, however, was not our safety, but the manner in which such threats were being handled in the post-Columbine world we live in.

Case in point: Two weeks after Kelley's arrest, a commotion was caused among faculty and some parents when a student wore an "I Support Kelley" T-shirt to school. Never mind that the shirt was referring to singer Kelly Osborne. The new policy at school seemed to be panic first and ask questions later.

Would Kelley have violently killed classmates and teachers from her own high school? We will never know. Personally, I would like to believe she wouldn't have, that her threats were hollow and made in the heat of emotion. She made a mistake, however, by putting her threats on paper. They became real, and authorities became involved.

Was I scared when my boyfriend frantically called me and told me

> **For Real?**
> Did you know that **Kelly Osborne** sings the theme song to *O Grady* on teen TV network, The N?

> **HOW ABOUT YOU?**
>
> A lot of teens say that they get a **bad rap** and that people **expect** them to do **bad stuff** just because they're teenagers. Do you think this is the case? How does this kind of thinking make *you* feel?

there had been a planned school shooting? Absolutely. I remember turning on the local news to see swarms of cop cars outside my school, transfixed by the breaking news report. It seemed so unreal, as though it should have been happening to some other school—anywhere but here.

It was only later as the facts came out that any of us were able to think rationally about it. And it's interesting to realize what doesn't get publicized on the news and in the paper. Kelley had been held back because of a learning problem, and as a result she was a year or two older than everyone else in her grade. Those close to her knew that she had family problems and was on medication for her mood swings.

No one seemed to care about that, however. All you have to do is say the words "school shooting," and people become so caught up in fear that they don't even listen to the rest of the story.

In this post-September 11th world we live in, sometimes fear overpowers rational thinking. Most students are now afraid to even say the word "gun" on campus or type the word "bomb" into an Internet search engine for fear they will be accused of committing a crime. Caution is a necessity, but when precaution turns into misguided fear and panic, we have a problem.

Instead of being remembered as a troubled, confused student in need of guidance, Kelley Kaminski will always be remembered as the "psycho" who wanted to blow up our school. Amidst our fear of safety and even public dissention,

CONSIDER THIS . . .

While more and more teens are taking **medication** to treat **depression**, experts are now realizing that these drugs may actually **increase suicidal thoughts** for some teens.

we have overlooked the facts of the story, satisfied with believing the rumors that spread like wildfire around the school in the days after the incident.

Franklin Delano Roosevelt once said, "We have nothing to fear but fear itself." I wonder what FDR would think of the world we are living in today, where our media focuses on the negative and often fails to present unbiased stories.

Seen It?

Michael Moore's documentary, *Bowling for Columbine*, looks at the culture of **fear** in our **society**, with a focus on the deadly teen shooting at Columbine High School in 1999.

A week ago, Kelley Kaminski was sentenced to an intensive seven-month probation. She was only seventeen years old.

People usually tend to fear what they don't know or don't understand. Now, weeks after Kelley's arrest, many people don't remember what counts she was even charged on. Some don't even know if she was convicted or not. All they know is that Basha High School is where that girl was arrested, and "Dude, she was gonna shoot kids and teachers and stuff."

Yes, I am concerned about the increase in school violence in recent years.

I am terrified, however, about living in a country where fear continues to motivate our actions and dominate our minds.

Sarah Sacco, Age 17

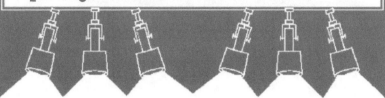

Spotlight On ... SCHOOL VIOLENCE

What is it that makes some teenagers snap under the pressure and violently act out against other students and teachers? Most people believe that violent teens have one of the following factors: low self-worth, feeling the need to gain attention and/or being the victim of abuse as a child.

And while school is still the safest place for teens to be, rumors about possible violence should be taken seriously. Here's how you can help to prevent a violent situation at your school:

- Start with yourself—don't give in to violence of any kind or carry a weapon.
- Immediately report any suspicious activity or violent behavior to an adult.
- Get involved. Join a Student Crime Watch at your school, or set one up if there isn't one.

WHERE DO YOU STAND?

Is fear a big part of your life?

Answer "yes" or "no" to these questions and find out:

___ YES   You check your date book every week to make
___ NO   sure you don't miss anyone's birthday.

___ YES   You try to convince your parents to change your
___ NO   vacation plans so that they don't involve flying.
           The thought of getting on a plane has you pretty
           psyched out.

___ YES   You insist on watching the local news every night,
___ NO   wanting to keep tabs on all the accidents and
           violent events happening in your city.

___ YES   You ask your mom to drive on surface streets
___ NO   rather than the highway whenever possible
           because you know that the chances of a serious
           car accident at 35 miles an hour are much
           slimmer than at 60.

___ YES   You can't seem to turn off your radar of being
___ NO   on the lookout for suspicious packages and
           people whenever you're in a public place.

___ YES   You decide to remove any heavy objects hung
___ NO   above your bed so that if there's an earthquake,
           you don't have to worry about them falling on
           your head.

If you answered yes to at least two of these questions, then
you are in danger of letting fearful thoughts consume you.

SEPTEMBER 11, 2001, WILL BE REMEMBERED as the day
that life as we knew it was forever changed. No matter what our
relationship with New York City and the Twin Towers or Washington,
D.C. and the Pentagon, the events of that day affected, and continues to affect, every American. Some of us grew angry, while others
were filled with despair. Others were terrified, while others bravely
took the opportunity to stand up and make a difference.

My own reaction was probably a combination of the above.
I had lived in New York City for most of my adult life, and the
events of that day hit close to home. So when I visited New York
just weeks after that terrible day, I can clearly remember sensing
a new energy in the city. And it wasn't one of fear or anger. It was
overwhelmingly an energy of hope, of kindness, of respect. It was
clear that the city, and even the nation at large, had been somehow
brought together . . . united in our pain and support for those who
had suffered incredible losses.

Now, nearly five years later, one has to wonder—where did
all of that positive momentum go? How can we hang on to the
goodwill and sense of community that we all experienced following
September 11th? The next two essays provide two different
per-spectives about how this tragedy had an impact and attempt
to answer the question, *What should we all take away from this
painful experience?*

The Day We Lost So Much

September 11th. I'll never forget the day. I went into the kitchen to eat my breakfast, and I saw my parents' eyes fixed on the television screen. I looked up to see what was so important, and I saw two planes half-hidden in those Twin Towers. To be honest, my initial reaction was not fear . . . it was confusion. I was only eleven at the time, and frankly I didn't even know what the Twin Towers were.

For Real?

When the **Twin Towers** were first opened in 1970 and 1972, they were the tallest buildings in the world until the **Sears Tower** in Chicago eclipsed them in 1973.

I ended up going to school, and everyone was talking about it. And, just like my parents that morning, everyone's eyes were fixed on the television screens. There was one girl at my school whose mother was in New York for a business trip. At first, she wasn't worried, but after everyone made such a big deal about it, she started to get scared. (As it turned out, her mother was fine—she ended up treating victims at a nearby hospital.)

At school, the teachers were trying to act calm for us, but we all knew something was very wrong. And then we saw it. The first tower came crashing down to the ground. Then the second followed. There

For Real?

Many schools first purchased **televisions** for the **classroom** in early 1949 so students could watch the live inauguration of President Harry Truman.

was so much to be done—bodies to be found, debris to be picked up. But what impacted me the most were the people on the news asking about their missing family members. People's lives were suddenly, and forever, changed.

HOW ABOUT YOU?

It's a day none of us will ever forget. Do you remember what you were doing when you first heard that the **Twin Towers** and the **Pentagon** had been **attacked**?

Since that day, I feel like many of us are still searching for an answer, wanting those missing bodies found, wanting the Towers restored like the whole thing never happened. Every time we see an image of New York City, there's something missing. And now I realize what I have lost . . . what everyone has lost. But the truth is, we're *never* going to get it back. We can never go back to that day, and it seems useless that people are always trying to put the blame on someone else.

"He didn't do his job!"

"No one took it seriously!"

"Why weren't they there when it happened?"

CONSIDER THIS . . .

Right after **September 11th**, people everywhere joined together in support of the victims' families and to help each other **deal** with the **tragedy**. Imagine how much good could come out of it if everyone continued to treat each other with that much support *all* of the time!

We keep fighting and blaming each other, but don't you think that the victims need a little more respect than that? Maybe I'm just a "confused teenager" and don't understand why finding the answers to all the questions is so important. But if I don't understand, then why am I here, writing this, thinking of all those lives lost, praying for those families instead of blaming someone for what happened? Pointing fingers won't change the past. But helping the families, remembering the Twin Towers in their glory, and smiling in the face of despair just might change the future. What would *you* rather do?

Jane Concha, Age 15

Looking Back

September 11, 2001, came plummeting into my world like a tidal wave. The raging water uprooted the nation I loved and the life I had lived. And with it thousands of innocent lives, their hopes and dreams for the future, the Manhattan skyline and other historic landmarks I cherished, and a country's hope for everlasting peace and stability ended. Yet there were people left behind to find light from underneath the rubble. People who will be forever haunted by the memory of September 11, 2001. People like me.

CONSIDER THIS . . .

In the wake of national disasters like **9/11**, the deadly **tsunami** in Asia in 2004 and **Hurricane Katrina**, teens everywhere are getting involved where it counts. Not only are **teens volunteering** their time and energy to existing organizations—they're **raising the bar** and creating their own.

Even now it is hard to envision my life before the tragedy, a life before brigades of police officers patrolled every street corner, a life before I learned the whereabouts of the Middle East, a life before the war and the countless casualties and "weapons of mass destruction." Sometimes I forget that I'm not forty years old, that it's not up to me to watch the news or read the paper or to worry—to worry and fret so much that I can't sleep at night.

For Real?

Perhaps in part because of **beefed-up security** in New York City since 9/11, NYC has the lowest crime rate for a large city in the country. Trailing behind it are: San Diego, Los Angeles, Philadelphia, Las Vegas, Houston, San Antonio, Phoenix, Detroit, and, ranked most dangerous, Dallas.

Yet, to live the life I led before September 11, 2001, seems impossible. The attacks still haunt me in my dreams. And when the events of that morning creep up on me time and time again in the dark, I'm taken aback with the same grim disbelief as if the shock has never sunk in. And maybe it hasn't.

HOW ABOUT YOU?

How have the events of September 11th **changed** how **you** view the world?

The dark shadows that creep carelessly around my bedroom walls in the dead of night and the sudden noises that now seem to flood my life bring back memories I try to forget, and fill my heart with fear of the unknown and the unseen. I am scared that something is going to happen. And, even worse, I don't know what that something is going to be.

Even now, when an airplane flies by on a sultry summer night, my mood changes as quickly as the plane passes. It seems that I have never gotten over my fear of planes. It has been years since I boarded one as a passenger. Sometimes as I sit in my backyard and stare up at the serene sky, my eyes toy with my greatest fear. It always seems as if the airplane in the sky is unexpectedly plunging toward the ground, or fly-ing too low toward a nearby building.

Sometimes I'm ashamed to feel afraid. I know that there are American soldiers stationed in every corner of the world who have risked everything to make sure that I'm safe. And in being afraid, I feel like I am taking their sacrifice for granted, although deep inside I know that I value their noble effort above all else.

I know that September 11th has ruined lives and directly affected my friends. And though the attacks have left an everlasting impact on my heart, I feel guilty. I have been more fortunate than most, and some say that I have nothing to

> **Address Book**
>
> **YouthNOISE** is a great Web site geared for teens, encouraging them to make noise and change their world. Check it out at *www.youthnoise.com.*

complain about (and sometimes I couldn't agree more). Yet, I know that everything that September 11th has taught me, all the life lessons I have learned from the courage and strength of others, I will carry with me into the future.

Paulina Karpis, Age 14

OUTSIDE THE BOX

Are you fearful of things that are beyond your control? If you feel like your fears are starting to take over your life, here are some strategies for coping:

- The next time you're feeling really afraid, stop and figure out what it is you're saying to yourself to make you feel this way. Are your thoughts <u>rational</u>?
- When you're feeling afraid and going to a bad place in your head, try to <u>change the thought</u>. Focus on a memory or place that makes you feel happy and calm.
- Realize that there are some things that are out of your control, and if you can't control it, there's no point in worrying about it.
- Avoid hanging out with people or being in situations that bring out feelings of fear in you.

WHERE DO YOU STAND?

Have the events of 9/11 changed you?
Have you noticed any of these changes?

You are more compassionate about the plight of others, and go out of your way to treat everyone like a human being and try to see things from other points of view.

- THAT'S ME   (0 points)
- ME, SOME OF THE TIME   (1 point)
- NOT ME AT ALL   (2 points)

You know that the future is in the hands of your generation, and you feel more inspired than ever to make a positive impact on the world.

- THAT'S ME   (0 points)
- ME, SOME OF THE TIME   (1 point)
- NOT ME AT ALL   (2 points)

You are more interested in learning about world events and understanding different cultures and religions so you can have a better sense of why things happened and how to prevent them in the future.

- THAT'S ME   (0 points)
- ME, SOME OF THE TIME   (1 point)
- NOT ME AT ALL   (2 points)

You volunteer more of your personal time for organizations that are doing important work, feeling a need to make a difference now.

- THAT'S ME   (0 points)
- ME, SOME OF THE TIME   (1 point)
- NOT ME AT ALL   (2 points)

As a way of coming to terms with the tragedy, you do your best to live in the moment and make every day count.

- THAT'S ME   (0 points)
- ME, SOME OF THE TIME   (1 point)
- NOT ME AT ALL   (2 points)

Add up your points:

0–3 = I'm a completely different person.

4–7 = I've made some small, but important changes.

8–10 = I'm the same as I've always been.

IF YOU WATCH THE EVENING NEWSCAST, then you know that bad news is everywhere. From terrorist attacks to tsunamis to the avian bird flu pandemic scare, it's easy to get caught up in all the fear and think that everything is just *bad*.

But the interesting thing is, sometimes it takes a scare to jolt us back into the world of the living, to remind ourselves that every day is a day to get out and live our lives. That's the lesson the author of this next essay learned when she had to confront a fear of her own.

Recovering from My Own Epidemic

"School will be suspended temporarily for safety from Atypical Pneumonia."

I couldn't believe it. One of my worst nightmares was coming true. I gazed in shock at the paper notice that was to change the days ahead.

It was springtime in Hong Kong, and there was a lot of fuss about the so-called Atypical Pneumonia, which was later renamed "SARS" or "Severe Acute Respiratory Syndrome." As a result, my classmates and I were gradually shoved into a mist of confusion and fear.

For Real?
During the **SARS** outbreak of 2003, more than 8,000 people in the world contracted SARS, and 774 died.

"Wear your mask," demanded a teacher.

"Go wash your hands," ordered another teacher.

Yet another said, "Don't touch each other like that."

I was sick of it all—not sick like I needed to rest and take pills, but sick in my heart and brain . . . a mental ache. Why was this happening? What exactly was going on? Why was everything chang-

HOW ABOUT YOU?

How would you spend your time if you were **forced** to stay home from school?

ing so quickly? Those were the questions that kept running through my mind when my fifth-grade teacher bid me farewell. I never thought I would see him again.

Before SARS came along, things were already not going well for me. Although I loved school, I was afraid to reveal my true spirit. I didn't have the courage to stand up and participate. Worse, I was such a slow writer that I had to work hard well past midnight every night just to finish my work. I hated my life. I couldn't truly love myself. I was stressed out and depressed, sometimes letting my frustration out in tears, other times by throwing tantrums. So being imprisoned by the SARS epidemic at home just made things worse. In looking back, the way I felt stuck at home represented the things I felt in my life in general—isolation, monotony, despair.

Health conditions in the city kept on deteriorating, and soon the struggle to live through the epidemic gripped us all. The news listed the dead every day to the song "We Shall Overcome." I kept on wondering, *What will I do if something happens to me or my family?* Surely the fate for everyone in Hong Kong was already destined.

"Clean up your room if you have nothing to do," my mom suggested.

I obeyed, going through everything in a drawer. That is what caused me to look back on happier times and question why I was feeling so down. *What is the life that you want?* I asked myself.

For Real?

The lyrics to the song "We Shall Overcome" came from a 1900 gospel song called "I'll Overcome Someday." It eventually became the anthem to the **Civil Rights Movement** in the mid-1900s.

Freedom, a reason to be on Earth and, most of all, happiness. So why don't you live the life that you want? Why have you been coping with a life you can't love? I thought.

Eventually, the SARS epidemic was brought under control, and life slowly began to resume normally again. But I knew I would never be the same. It didn't happen overnight, but as soon as school started back up, I opened the doors to the life that I've always wanted. All I needed to do was to take a step forward. I learned to never be reluctant about doing what I want to do. I became the new funny, silly, optimistic girl my friends recognize me as. I began to feel thankful for even the smallest things in my life. Even walking outdoors was a pleasure. It turns out that I was the only one holding myself back, neglecting little things and waiting for big ones. My days of SARS taught me this. After all, in order to drive a car, the engine must be running. And in life, you've got to be the one to turn the key.

Eri Mizobe, Age 13

OUTSIDE THE BOX

If you find that you're unhappy or not living your life the way you want to, try some of these ideas to discover what truly brings you joy:

- Make a list of things that you enjoy doing, and write or think about what it is about each item that love so much.
- Flip through magazines and cut out images that you appeal to you, like a view you hope to see one day out of your window or an animal that makes you smile. Put these images in a folder or notebook to keep you inspired.
- When you discover things that you enjoy, research and explore opportunities to expand on that interest. For example, if you love animals, see if you can volunteer at a local animal shelter or zoo.

I CAUGHT AN EPISODE OF *OPRAH* the other day. (By now you've probably realized that I watch *Oprah* a lot.) The episode was about the movie *Crash*, which deals with the serious issues of racism and prejudice. Interviews with the cast and screening of clips from the film were followed by a Q&A period where audience members talked about things they had done or said that might be considered a form of racism.

What I loved about that episode was that it showed how blurry the lines of prejudice can be, and how many of us may think prejudicial thoughts without even being aware that they're there. Think about it. Have you ever crossed the street to walk on another sidewalk because someone of a different race from you was

approaching? Have you ever made assumptions about someone
from a different cultural background that were based on
stereotypes?

The author of this next poem was pondering these same
questions when she wrote "Prejudice." In writing this poem, she
hopes to show people that prejudice is a negative thing, and that
people should be regarded as *people*, no matter what race,
religion, gender or ethnicity.

Prejudice

My eyes meet hers
I see her dark skin, her dark clothes
But do I really see?

I judge her by her skin, her face
Difference is the brother of
   inferiority
I hear her voice—the tone, the
   expression
But do I really listen?
Do I really hear?
Do I really care?

Read It?

Jacqueline Woodson's YA
novel *If You Come Softly*
tells the story of two teens—
Jeremiah, who is black, and
Ellie, who is white—and
what happens when they
fall in love.

The content of what she is saying
Makes no difference to me
These same words came out of my mouth yesterday
This fact will be disregarded

I am not in contact with an individual,

Rather, a representative from a different culture

When I look at people as people, *really* look . . .

Disregard their ethnicity . . .

Then

And only then

Will I really, truly see.

Brooke Raphalian, Age 14

For Real?

The U.S. is truly one big **melting pot**.
In 2005, the U.S. population was:

69.1% = White
12.9% = Black
12.6% = Hispanic
4.2% = Asian
1.0% = Amero-Indian
.2% = Hawaiian and Pacific Islander

Take the Quiz:

HOW DO YOU COPE WITH WHAT'S GOING ON IN THE WORLD OUT THERE?

1. The U.S. is involved in a conflict overseas that you just don't agree with and you're afraid of a draft that could affect your older brother. What do you do?

___ A. You know that the most important thing you can do is to make your voice heard. You get involved in student rallies against the war and stand up for what you believe in.

___ B. You are scared of your brother being drafted, but feel powerless to do anything about it, so you just hope for the best.

___ C. You get filled with anger at what's going on and begin to resent anyone who isn't against the conflict.

2. When a plot for a school shooting is uncovered at a school district a few miles away, the administration at your school goes into overdrive for fear of the same thing happening there. Suddenly, mega metal detectors are put in place, cell phones are prohibited, and all Internet searches in the library are monitored. What do you do?

___ A. You are all for being cautious, but you feel like what's going on is way overboard. You start a petition at your school to have the new measures taken away and start a student-led watchdog organization charged with keeping the school safe.

___ B. You feel like your school is going over the top, but you can't help but feel like they have a good point in being so proactive, so you just go along with it without question.

___ C. You think the whole security thing is a big joke and roll your eyes every time your metal pencil carrier sets off the alarm. You act out in class and at school events with your friends to voice your frustration.

3. It's New Year's Eve, and the U.S. government has raised the terror alert warning one level for New York City, asking citizens to be especially vigilant. You live in Little Rock, Arkansas, more than a thousand miles away. How do you spend your New Year's Eve?

 ___ A. You know that while being cautious is always a good idea, there are some things that are beyond your control. You also realize the chances of something happening to you are microscopic, so you go on with your evening as planned.

 ___ B. You still want to hang out with your friends, but can't help but feel a little nervous about going out as you originally planned. You convince your group of friends to do a party at your house and then try to forget what's going on in the outside world.

 ___ C. Every time the terror alert warning is raised, you feel a strong urge to lock yourself up inside the house and hide out until it goes back down. This New Year's Eve will be no different.

4. A natural disaster on the scale of Hurricane Katrina hits the southwestern United States. Thousands of people are killed and injured, and countless others are homeless. You've been watching the whole thing unfold on CNN. What do you do?

 ___ A. You know that even if you're miles away, you can still find a way to contribute and help. You mobilize your friends to get donations from local businesses to send to victims to help them get back on their feet.

 ___ B. You feel bad for a few days while the plight of those affected is being broadcast on the evening news, but as soon as the coverage dwindles down, so does your interest.

___ C. You can't seem to turn off the TV, enthralled by the images coming through on the screen, but instead of finding a way to help the victims, you go into your own cocoon, fearful that the same thing might happen to you and your family one day.

5. A major political scandal has the whole government in an upheaval. Even though you're not old enough to vote yet, you know that what happens in the government today is going to impact your future. How do you handle it?

___ A. You've got strong opinions about what's happening, and you want to make your voice heard. You write an editorial to the newspaper speaking up about your viewpoint, knowing it's never too early to get involved.

___ B. You want to take a stand about what's going on, but feel powerless to do so. If you can't even get your parents to take your point of view seriously, why would anyone else?

___ C. You find all of this political mumbo jumbo beyond depressing and decide to completely zone out of what's going on. Why deal with this kind of stuff until you have to?

So, how do you cope with what's happening out there? If your answers were . . .

Mostly A's = You know that even as an individual teen you have power, and you take the opportunity to exercise that power whenever you can. You can truly change your world!

Mostly B's = While you are disheartened by a lot of what's happening in the world, you tend to take a more passive approach to making sense of it all. You have an interest in making a difference, but aren't sure how or where to start. Try getting involved in something that sparks your interest and see how far it takes you.

Mostly C's = You'd rather avoid the issues that frustrate you than do anything about them because you feel powerless to make any difference. You might find, however, that picking a cause and throwing yourself into it will empower you in ways you never imagined.

CHAPTER 7

PRESSURE

Pressure is everywhere: the pressure to be like everyone else, the pressure to be different, the pressure to excel, the pressure to be liked, the pressure to look a certain way. There's the pressure we place on ourselves, and the pressure that others thrust upon us. But no matter where the pressure's coming from, we need to find a way to handle it. This chapter explores pressure from different angles and shares some ideas for coming to grips.

IF YOU READ THE STATISTICS, you know that for most teens, it's not a matter of *if* you will be pressured into drinking and trying drugs—it's a matter of *when*. Taken one step further, the real matter is *what* you will do when and if it happens. Here's a story of how one girl faced the pressure and very real temptation, and ultimately said "no."

HOW ABOUT YOU?

Do you know any kids at school who regularly **use drugs**? Why do **you** think they use them?

Vicodin

Everyone has their own group of friends. Mine was pretty much drug-free. A couple of kids had tried drugs once or twice, but not enough to be an addict—except Pam. She was a beautiful and sweet girl when I first met her. She had dark brown hair and dark brown eyes—my idea of perfection.

After we became friends, Pam began to lose her glow. She was spacier, and her beautiful face began to look less like a model's and more like a hillbilly's. She was becoming less and less like the wonderful Pam I had met a year before. One day at lunch she asked if she could borrow a few dollars. I said sure because I had extra money on me. She thanked me, told me she'd pay me back and walked away.

A day or so later, Pam walked up to me with a mischievous grin on her face. Her hand was folded into a fist as she gave me a hug and shoved her fisted hand into my back pocket. She pulled her hand out of my pocket as she released me from the hug. As I walked away from her, I felt something inside my back pocket. I went into the bathroom and found a pill in a plastic Baggie. I was extremely surprised because I don't do drugs. I looked at the pill, marked *M360*, and I couldn't tell what it was. I was so confused as to why she'd given this to me—I kept it in my back pocket until I got home.

For Real?

Vicodin is a serious pain reliever with lots of negative side effects, including:
• dizziness • nausea
• anxiety • mood changes
• drowsiness • skin rashes

I decided to hide the large white pill in an old purse, and there it stayed for five months. It was actually extremely hard having it there. Just knowing I had the pill made me very curious and tempted to try it.

One night, I got out the pill which I had found out was Vicodin, and took it down to the bathroom. Suddenly, I knew exactly what to do. I looked at it and saw pure evil . . . Pam's seduction and torture. I stared until I couldn't look at it anymore, and then I dumped it into the toilet.

I realized that I don't need a chemical to have fun. I have the greatest friends a girl could ask for, and Pam has her drugs. I've got no interest in trying her seductive substances. Vicodin just isn't my thing.

Bridgett Van Veezak, Age 14

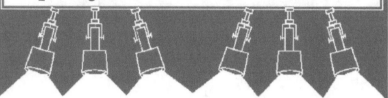

Spotlight On ... TEENS & DRUGS

While it might not seem that way from the news, drug use among teens is actually on the decline. But that doesn't mean it still isn't a major problem for teens everywhere. Here are a few interesting statistics:

- While marijuana is the most common drug used by students, its use has declined in the last few years.
- 9.3% of high-school seniors have tried or used Vicodin.
- The drug use that *has* increased is that of inhalants, which are things like nail polish remover and paint thinner.
- Every 24 hours, more than 15,000 teens will try drugs for the first time.

If you're concerned that a friend might have a problem with drugs, ask yourself these questions:

- Does he or she rely on drugs to have fun?
- Is your friend keeping secrets from you?
- Is he or she performing differently in school?

If you answered "yes" to any of these questions, your friend might be struggling with a drug problem.

For more information, check out the Web site Snappy at *www2.edc.org/snappy/students.html* or call the Youth Crisis Hotline at 1-800-HIT-HOME.

OUTSIDE THE BOX

If you're getting pressured by someone to try drugs, here's how to say no:

- Change the subject or suggest an alternative plan.
- If you're able to, call your parents on your cell and use a prearranged code word to let them know you're in a bad spot. When your parents come and get you, you can make them look like the heavies and still save face with your "friends."
- Say "no" and mean it. If your friends realize you're not going to change your mind, they'll stop pressuring you.

WHERE DO YOU STAND?

Do you know the truth about drugs and drinking?

1. ⑦ ⑦   Girls are more easily affected by alcohol than boys are.

2. ⑦ ⑦   Beer and wine are safer drinks to try than booze because they're not as potent.

3. ⑦ ⑦   One out of every five teens has used an inhalant at least once.

4. ⑦ ⑦   One of the biggest causes of teenage drinking i boredom.

5. ⑦ ⑦   All of the press about beer drinking being dangerous is just an attempt by adults to get teens to stop partying. The worst thing that can happen from drinking beer is a bad hangover.

1. TRUE: While many different factors influence how alcohol affects the body, including weight and how full a person's stomach is, as a rule, girls are usually more affected by alcohol than boys.

2. FALSE: While beer and wine don't have the same percentage of alcohol as hard liquor like vodka, drinking too much of any kind of alcohol is extremely dangerous and can be fatal.

3. TRUE: 20% of teens have tried dangerous inhalants, an especially alarming statistic when you consider that even one time can be fatal.

4. TRUE: Teen drinking can be attributed to, among other things, boredom, curiosity and low self-esteem.

5. FALSE: Drinking beer can be deadly, especially when the drinker is participating in "binge drinking," and the liver isn't able to flush the alcohol out of the body efficiently enough. Eventually, the body just can't handle the amount of alcohol in the system, and coma or death can result.

ONE OF THE THINGS I FIND MOST INTERESTING ABOUT LIFE is how every bad thing that happens in our lives has the capacity to turn itself around into a positive thing. Think about it. The people who come to your school to lead assemblies on the importance of saying "no" to drugs or drinking and driving are usually people who've suffered the negative side effects of their actions. They've taken the opportunity to turn their experience around so it could benefit others. The next time you experience something bad, why not try thinking about what would happen if you turned it around so others could learn something, too?

The Power of a Voice

A girl, 14, with makeup
    covering her face.
She had pom-poms and
    popularity to hide her
    disgrace.
Everyone sees a teenage girl
    who has it all.
Little do they know she is
    suffering from drugs and
    alcohol.

CONSIDER THIS . . .

Popularity isn't all it's cracked up to be. Many "popular" teens admit that they feel **tons of pressure** to live up to the "ideal" when it comes to **looks, fashion** and **being cool**. Many of these popular kids do things that they don't want to do, like drink alcohol, because it relieves them of some of the pressure they feel.

Head cheerleader, class
    president, the person everyone wants to be,
But none of them were as unhappy and dissatisfied as she.
Between her broken family and her eating disorder,
She found the answer was to make her life shorter.

Writing her suicide note was
   the hardest thing she could do.
The only words that came out
   were "I love you."
As she picked up the pills, her
   stomach cramped and her
   mind began to blur.
When her mother walked in, her
   words started to slur.

> **For Real?**
> Some researchers
> believe that up to **25%**
> of today's **teens** think
> about committing
> **suicide** at least once.

Her mom didn't say a word, just gave her a hug.
And for the first time she didn't think about sadness or
   a drug.
From the love and compassion they both shared.
She knew she'd be okay because
   somebody cared.

As her friends started to buy
   drugs, using every penny,
She realized her voice seemed to
   be the echo of many.
Everyone was thinking about
   drinking and drugs,
Slowly they were turning into alcoholic thugs.

> **Address Book**
> If you know someone who's
> considering **suicide**, or
> you're considering it your-
> self, get help **now**. Call the
> *National Hopeline Network*
> at **1-800-SUICIDE.**

Now that she is over her unhappy days,
She works to help others that had her same phase.
She learned many things about making the right choice.
Between helping, loving and the power of a voice.

Jessica Ekstrom, Age 14

Spotlight On ... PEER PRESSURE

What is peer pressure anyway? It's when your peers, or people around you who are your age, try to get you to do something that you might not do otherwise, like smoke, drink, cheat, gang up on someone, and so on. We all face it from time to time, and it can be hard to stand up to, especially if the people pressuring you are your friends or people you hope to hang out with.

Peer pressure comes in all shapes and sizes, from not-so-serious issues like wearing a certain kind of clothing just because it's "in," to more serious and possibly dangerous issues like drinking at a party because you don't want to stand out.

Standing up to peer pressure is tough, but it's not impossible. It does take a little planning and a lot of confidence. The next time you feel like you're doing something for the wrong reasons, ask yourself this question: *If I had my own way, would I still be doing this?* If the answer is "no," you might want to reevaluate the situation, and the peers who are leaning on you.

SOMETIMES, THE WAY WE IMAGINE THINGS SHOULD HAPPEN and the way they actually do happen are two completely different things. If you're a laid-back, go-with-the-flow kind of person, then this is no problem—you can roll with the punches and adapt to the way things unfold. But if you're even a little like me, and by that I mean a *Type A personality*, when things don't go the way you hoped you get seriously thrown off.

I wish I could say that I've completely dealt with this issue, but that would be a lie. Things with me usually have to be "just so," and if they're not, watch out. But every now and then someone reminds me that the Earth won't stop spinning if I make a typo in an article I'm writing. Yes, daylight will break once again, even if I do skip a Sunday morning run because my bed is just too warm and comfy. Sometimes, if we just stop and ask ourselves what's the worst thing that can happen if things don't go as we planned, we'll realize that trying to be perfect just isn't worth all the trouble.

THE WORD

A **Type A personality** is one where the person is driven by a need to do things quickly and well, and want to have control over just about everything.

The Perfect Demon

When I was eight, I sat in my third-grade classroom in tears, inconsolable because I'd put the wrong spelling of the word "horse" on my poster. Crying for hours, I pushed my teacher to the point where she finally called my mom. She told my mom what had happened in class, and even suggested

For Real?

Today's teens are experiencing **stress symptoms** like sleeping problems, headaches and skin breakouts at younger and younger ages, possibly because today's youth are more **overbooked** than any generation before them.

I get some counseling. She said I was too stressed. Think about it: At eight years old, I was *too stressed*. There's something very wrong with that picture. What problems does an eight-year-old have to deal with? I was already showing signs of a very serious disease . . . a curse built into my personality.

I needed to be perfect. Flawless. Nothing but absolute precision was acceptable to me. I got mad if I got a 95% on a quiz. I wasn't happy . . . *ever*. I always knew I could do better. When I got an assignment back, my first move was to check and see what I did wrong. I needed to learn it. I needed to have 100% next time. I needed to be perfect.

And I continued that way for years and years. I pushed myself to ace everything. Beat everyone. Be the best in every way I could think of. I wanted to be the ultimate human being. I wanted to be up so high that no one could touch me. I wanted to be deemed unbeatable. That's all I wanted. That's not asking too much, is it?

CONSIDER THIS . . .

Learning how to deal with being **less than perfect** is a good idea. Even if you're used to **excelling**, there comes a time in everyone's life when there will be someone better at something **you** do.

I got to the point where life became hideous. It was filled with disappointments due to human error. I continued to break into undying tears over the smallest things—low grades, missed homework assignments . . . basically everything. I tried to break away from my curse, but to no avail. I was trapped. My obsession with being perfect led me down a road of distress, filled with homework assignments, studying, rushing through tests so I could be the first one done and basically making myself much more stressed than anyone needed to be.

CONSIDER THIS . . .

Perfect grades aren't the only thing that matters when it comes to getting into college and landing good jobs. **Involvement** in extracurricular activities, interests and hobbies plays a role, too.

That's when I began to notice something about one of my friends. She had always been a lot like me, but she was even more extreme in her perfectionism. For example, occasionally, she would miss swim practice to work on a big project due the next day. I didn't really think that much of it. But it got worse. Progressively, I saw her less and less until by the end of the school year, I realized I hadn't seen her in over a month. But I had noticed that when I talked with her, she was stressed, on the verge of tears, fighting to be the same thing I wanted to be: *perfect.* She was tearing herself apart over every little thing. She was constantly worried and couldn't ever seem to rclax. I felt bad for her.

Then one day, when my mom and I went to pick up my friend for swim practice, I saw the tears flowing freely down her face as she tore herself up over an essay that she was afraid she might not finish. It was due the next day, and she had all night to do it. Her mom said that she probably couldn't go to swim practice that night, so we said good-bye and left her and her mom to figure out the essay problem. On the drive home, my mom said, "And I thought *you* were a perfectionist." Now I'd always known that I put a lot of pressure on myself to be perfect, but I never realized what I was doing to myself—what a perfectionist actually is.

Then it clicked. I finally made the connection. I was in no better shape than my friend. I was forcing myself to give up all of my free time to be perfect. I was striving toward an unattainable goal. I was torturing myself with an ideal that was impossible to reach. And so, little by little, I relaxed. I realized that getting an 80% instead of 100% every once in a while wouldn't kill me, and I accepted the lower grades when they came. I learned to let go of studying all the time and instead learn the skill of quick memorization right before class. I began to grasp the concept that it is only human to make a mistake, and I learned how to forgive my own. Although it was hard, I stopped expecting perfect scores. Basically, I lowered my standards. My life needed to be more than work. More than worry. More than being perfect.

THE WORD

A **perfectionist** sets extremely high standards for himself or herself, often accepting nothing less than perfect in everything they do.

And so I changed. I laughed more, I smiled wider, and I worried less. I stopped letting my work plague my every thought and discovered the ability to tolerate my flawed human self. Ironically, though my grades suffered an initial drop, they rebounded to being higher than ever before.

But I know, underneath the surface, I still have to be careful. A demon still lurks in my subconscious, pushing me to be perfect, pushing me to excel. His strength is immense; his expectations are high. He is the perfect demon, pulling me apart from the inside out, demanding perfection. I've come to terms with that, and I've learned how to deal with his constant nagging. But I do know that at any moment he could reemerge to take over. I have to fight him with every move I make and remember that everything is not a competition. Most importantly, though, I'm no longer in denial. I'm coping. Learning to deal.

"My name is Katelynn, and I am a perfectionist."

Katelynn Wilton, Age 16

Read It?

Kate Malone, the protagonist in Laurie Halse Anderson's book *Catalyst*, is a perfectionist.

OUTSIDE THE BOX

Are you a perfectionist? Do you get bummed out when you don't perform as well as you think you should? If so, hear this—perfection is just an illusion. You'll never be perfect, so why bother getting frustrated with yourself for being unable to do the impossible? Here are some ways to stop being a perfectionist:

- **Do the unexpected.** If you're a perfectionist about your appearance, go to the mall in your rattiest clothes and bed head and see how it feels.
- **Put things in perspective.** Read a story about the victims of Hurricane Katrina or watch a movie about the civil rights movement.
- **Be rational.** Play out what would happen if you weren't perfect all the time. Would it really be the end of the world?

WHERE DO YOU STAND?

Are you putting too much pressure on yourself?

Your partner in a big class project totally drops the ball. Do you redo her work so that you don't look bad?

- DEFINITELY (0 points)
- MAYBE (1 point)
- NOT AT ALL (2 points)

Your older brother was valedictorian of his class and president of the school's national honor society. Do you feel pressured to follow in his footsteps?

- DEFINITELY (0 points)
- MAYBE (1 point)
- NOT AT ALL (2 points)

Your sculpture gets second place in the county fair arts and crafts competition. Are you devastated that you didn't win the grand prize?

- DEFINITELY (0 points)
- MAYBE (1 point)
- NOT AT ALL (2 points)

You have a nasty case of the flu, but sacrifice your sleep to study for your big mid-term. Anything less than an A won't do.

- DEFINITELY (0 points)
- MAYBE (1 point)
- NOT AT ALL (2 points)

All of your friends are going skiing for the weekend, but you're in training for a volleyball tournament and want to get your practices in. Do you skip out on your friends?

- DEFINITELY (0 points)
- MAYBE (1 point)
- NOT AT ALL (2 points)

Add up your points:

0–3 = You have a lot of pressure weighing you down.
4–7 = You have high standards but know that there are things more important than being the best.
8–10 = You go with the flow and take things as they come.

Take the Quiz:
ARE YOU PREPARED
TO HANDLE PRESSURE ❓

1. You and your friends were excited about getting invited to a high-school party, but when you get there you see everyone is partying pretty hard. As soon as you get there, someone shoves a drink in your hand. You're not really into drinking and weren't prepared to be in this situation. How do you handle it?

   ___ A. It's your first senior party, and the last thing you want is to be labeled as a dork. You decide to join in . . . isn't that what being a teen is all about anyway?

   ___ B. You hold on to your cup, but don't actually drink any of the booze, trying not to stand out.

   ___ C. You put the drink down and pull your friend aside as soon as you get a chance, telling her that this really isn't your scene. You convince your friend to hit the road with you and go somewhere else.

2. You and your friends rent a limo to take you and your dates to the Homecoming Dance, but when you and your date step inside, you realize everyone is madly making out. You aren't sure that you are that into your date. What do you do?

   ___ A. You get in the limo and decide to go along with the crowd and make out with your date. It's just for a short ride anyway, and to protest in the limo might make you come off like a prude.

   ___ B. You and your date climb into the limo and make a joke about what's going on inside. You try to change everyone's focus by putting on some party music and starting a conversation with your friends.

_____ C. You ask your date if he wouldn't mind getting a ride with someone else to the dance—the limo feels a little crowded.

3. The biggest test of your life—the dreaded SAT—is coming up, and you have set a goal of getting a 1220 on your test, since that's the average score of students who are admitted to your first choice of colleges. You've got two weeks left before the test, and your stress level is starting to rise. How do you cope?

_____ A. Anything less than 1220 would be unacceptable to you, even though you only got a 1070 on the practice test you did online last month. You cram studying into every waking hour of your days until the big test.

_____ B. You are seriously stressed out about the whole thing. You start second-guessing your choices of colleges and come up with a back-up plan in case you don't make your mark.

_____ C. You know that being stressed isn't going to do anything to help your test score, so you focus on studying while making sure to take the time to get enough rest, eat well and relax in the weeks leading up to the test.

4. A close friend slips you a little pill one day while passing you a note. The note says, "Try when you're alone and want to feel really good." You didn't know your friend was experimenting with drugs, and you don't know what to do. What's your next step?

_____ A. You feel conflicted over what to do because if you don't try it, your friend will know it, and you don't want to look like a loser. You decide to break the pill in half and take it one night before you go to bed.

_____ B. You hold on to the pill, but don't take it. When your friend asks you what you thought, you tell her you haven't had a chance to try it yet, but when you do, you'll give her all the details.

___ C. You've got no interest in trying this pill, and you don't really care if your friend thinks you're a square for throwing it away. You tell your friend not to give you another pill ever again.

5. Your BFF has a huge crush on a guy in marching band, and when he asks her to a dance, she begs you to double date with his best friend. You don't think much of his best friend at all, but don't want to let your friend down either, especially because she's hounding you every night with calls asking what you're going to do. How do you handle it?

___ A. You may not like this guy very much, but you don't think it's worth letting your friend down, so you suck it up and go to the dance with the other guy, hoping the evening goes by quickly.

___ B. You agree to go to the dance with this guy, but as soon as you get there, you ditch him, opting to hang out with other friends instead.

___ C. You tell your friend that you're sorry, but you just aren't up for going to the dance with this guy, and suggest you and another date accompany the pair. You know that if she respects you as a friend, she'll understand your decision.

So, are you prepared to handle pressure when it comes your way? Give yourself 10 points for every A, 20 points for every B, and 30 points for every C:

50–70 points = Just a little bit of pressure placed on you, either by yourself or someone else, can make you burst like an over-inflated balloon. Find a way to handle pressure-filled situations before you're in them so when things come up, you have a plan for getting through them in style.

80–120 points = You usually know what you want, but don't always feel empowered to speak up when someone is putting the pressure on you. Instead, you tend to find a compromise that you can live with. The next time you're feeling pressure that feels uncomfortable, try speaking up and see how it feels. You just might find it's easier to speak up than it is to give in.

130–150 points = Bring it on! You know how you feel about things, and no amount of pressuring by anyone is going to get you to do something you don't want to do, even if it is that little voice inside your head pushing you to be perfect.

CHAPTER 8

FINDING YOUR VOICE

So, I think we can all agree by now that life can be tough. Life can be challenging. But does that mean we have to just put up with it and accept difficulties when they come along? No way. This next chapter is all about finding your voice and taking a stand.

THINK ABOUT SOMEONE YOU KNOW who you would consider to be as straight-laced as they come. Maybe it's an honor-roll student from school, or a goody-two-shoes from Sunday school. Can you believe that this person has ever done something that they're ashamed of? Do you find it hard to imagine that they've lied or cheated or stolen something or even purposefully hurt someone else's feelings? Well, unless they're from another planet, chances are your straight-laced acquaintance has a few skeletons in his or her closet. Yes, most likely they've messed up at least once . . . and *big* time. They wouldn't be human without these kinds of experiences.

But that's really what it's all about, isn't it? We all screw up from time to time. I think we do it so we can get another chance and learn about ourselves and how we fit in with the world. That's what I love about this next short piece, "Dear Future Destiny." In it, the author asks his future self to not turn its back on him for the mistakes he makes today. Because after all, he's only human.

Dear Future Destiny

Dear Future Destiny,

I hope you are kind to me. I hope you don't destroy my feelings and that you consider looking at things from every angle and every perspective, just as I would do to you. Please notice that I not only make mistakes, but I also learn from them and create wonderful things called *lessons*. Remember that I'm in your hands and if you drop me I will break. If I'm ever not myself, remind me that I'm a truly beautiful person inside and out. You're the future. When will you come my way? I do not know. But what I do know is that "someday" will soon become *today*.

Sincerely,

John

John Penny, Age 18

THE WORD

Destiny is the idea that the things that happen to us in the future are *fated* to happen. Do you believe in destiny?

OUTSIDE THE BOX

Are you up for doing a cool writing experiment? Pull out your journal or a piece of paper and try writing a letter to <u>your</u> future destiny. Here are some ideas to get you going:

- What is your biggest dream or goal for your future self?
- What do you hope your lifestyle will be like in the future?
- When you're older, how do you think you'll look back on the things you did as a teen?
- Are there things about yourself that you hope will be different in the future?
- If you could change one thing about yourself, what would it be?
- If you could keep one thing exactly the same in the future, what would it be?
- If you had one piece of advice for your future self, what would you say?

DO YOU REMEMBER THE FIRST TIME YOU HEARD someone being put down because of their skin color or ethnic background? Or maybe you were the one who was treated differently because of the way you look or who you are. How did it make you feel?

I'm a big believer in the idea that racism and prejudice really can be stopped in our lifetime. All it takes is each one of us to refuse to partici- pate—refuse to use language that puts others down, refuse to support friends who discriminate. It's up to us as individuals to *break the cycle*.

Read It?

Chris Crutcher's novel *Whale Talk* features a character named The Tao, who is part white, part black and part Japanese.

If Roses Can Be . . .

If roses can be
Yellow
Pink
Red
White
And still be roses

If hair can be
Red
Blonde
Brunette
Black
And still be hair

If eyes can be
Green
Blue
Brown
Hazel
And still be eyes

Then why can't humans be
Black
White
Hispanic
Asian
And still be accepted?

Why can't people be
Special
Different
Unique
Original
And still be people?

If roses can be
Yellow
Pink
Red
White
And still be roses . . .

For Real?

1% of the population has a condition called **heterchromia**, which means that each eye is a different color. Singer David Bowie and actor Kiefer Sutherland both have heterochromia.

CONSIDER THIS . . .

Maybe it's because of the popularity of the hit movie *Napoleon Dynamite*, but suddenly being a "band geek" is considered **cool**. In fact, students everywhere are showing their band-geek pride by wearing T-shirts that say things like "ORCH DORKS" with the name of their instrument on the back.

Lyssa Hoganson, Age 12

I REMEMBER A TIME WHEN I SO DESPERATELY WANTED to be a part of a certain clique at school. Even though I'd get close, somehow I was always "on the fringe" of being cool. Even when I would hang out with this group, I always felt like I didn't belong, like I was being tolerated because one of my friends was one of their own. I used to think that life would be perfect if they'd only fully accept me, but they never did.

I guess that for whatever reason, they didn't want me hanging around. And even though it hurt my feelings to be so obviously rejected by people I just about worshipped, deep down inside I knew I never would have fit in anyway. And making friends with people who didn't reject me was substantially easier because I could spend less time trying to impress them and fit in and more time being me.

Fitting In

I don't know why, but for some reason I always find myself changing to fit in with the cool crowd. Starting in fifth grade, I completely transformed myself so I could be a part of the "it clique"—a group of five sixth-grade girls who wore jeans and Limited Too tight T-shirts and played Truth or Dare with the boys in the woods. My main focus in life that year was to become one of them. When the leader of the group told me all I had to do was change my wardrobe to hang out with them, I jumped at the opportunity. On a three-hour spree at the air-conditioned mall, I bought jeans and fitted pants and T-shirts with sayings like "Princess," "Angel" and "Goddess" to

HOW ABOUT YOU?

What do **you** think of **racy, tight T-shirts** for girls with words on them like "Hot Chicks" or "Baby Doll"? Do you think they're sending a good or bad message?

replace the cotton dresses I had been wearing my whole life.

Without a trace of regret, I sauntered into school having completely ridden myself of the old "loser" me and ready to welcome the new "cool" me. The girls added me to their group, making the fabulous five a fabulous six. When one of them made an offhanded comment about my hair lacking shape, I cut angles and layers in it. Anything they wanted, I would get for them. Everything they said, I'd do. From an outsider's view, it may have looked like I was being used. Well, I was. But I was also benefiting from it in ways that overpowered the abuse.

After elementary school ended, my clique separated, as we were all attending different middle schools, and I was forced to start over. Although I had been considered "cool" at my sheltered private school, in actuality I knew nothing about popularity and style in the real public-school world. I was teased miserably. Random girls would ask me why my hair was so greasy ... my so-called best friend asked me why I didn't wear cover-up to conceal my acne. As I only wanted one thing—to be accepted and popular—I began my second major change.

CONSIDER THIS . . .

Even though many girls wear cover-up to hide their **acne**, wearing makeup with heavy oils can actually make skin problems **worse**.

I met a popular girl who let me be her friend. She also helped me transform. We worked out together—she did my makeup until I was a pro at it myself, and she taught me about fashion and lent me her clothes. Middle-school students are much more ruthless than elementary-school kids. My changes weren't happening quickly enough, and I wasn't being accepted as I knew I should be. This called for desperate measures. I began monitoring my diet so that all I would eat was one apple per day.

Seen It?

The movie *Love Don't Cost a Thing* (2003) stars Nick Cannon as a high-school outcast who becomes popular after paying a cool girl in school to pose as his girlfriend.

As the weight dropped, people were drawn to me. I hadn't been overweight before, but now I looked like the starving models all the girls strived to be. Now that I had acquired a beautiful best friend to get into trouble with, stylish clothing and a flawless physique, I was all set.

But as part of these new changes in my life, I lost my values. I had always been a good girl and followed the rules. I had promised myself not to smoke or do drugs. Alcohol was something I would never dream of tasting, and sexual activities beyond kissing were to be saved for marriage. Within a year, I broke all of these promises to myself. I never even thought about what I was doing—I was too swept up in the energy of the crowd and the encouragement of my best friend.

A year later, my connection to popularity was lost. My best friend and partner-in-crime and I broke up, leaving me alone as an overly made-up, skinny, lonely, lost girl.

The next few months were miserable. Having lost the energy to make myself look "good," I wore sweatpants and T-shirts to school. My eye makeup disappeared, and my hair went back to its natural wavy state. I had come to the conclusion that no one would want to talk to me now that I wasn't cool, but I couldn't have been more wrong. People who I had treated horribly made an effort to befriend me. Instead of partying and watching my drunk friends puke and get into bad situations with boys, I went out and watched movies and ate personal pizzas. The people who I had gossiped about were the ones to accept me as I really am. It was quite a lesson to learn.

Read It?

The science-fiction novel *The House of the Scorpion* by Nancy Farmer tells the story of Mateo, a clone, and his journey of self-discovery as he realizes what makes him tick.

When I finally broke down and was able to show the real me, I found true friends. I learned forgiveness from them. Friendship and life are not about who's wearing what or who is hooking up with whom or where the big party is. It's about loving people for their true selves and learning from their eccentricities and differences. Finally, I am able to express myself and be happy with who I am instead of always trying to fake it.

Liia Rudolph, Age 17

WHERE DO YOU STAND?

Are you making potentially bad choices?

Answer "yes" or "no" to these questions and find out:

___ YES You have a personal philosophy
___ NO   of "act now, think later." Why worry
         about the consequences when
         you're having so much fun?

___ YES You figure that most authority figures
___ NO   expect you to be a foolish teenager,
         and you don't want to disappoint
         them. Isn't that what youth is all
         about anyway?

___ YES When you defy your parents, you
___ NO   do things that you know they
         themselves did as teens. How can
         they be mad at you for following
         in their footsteps?

___ YES You know that you're only young
___ NO   once, and you don't want to be an
         adult and have any regrets about
         not doing this or that when you
         were younger.

___ YES You figure you'll try anything, good
___ NO   or bad, once . . . then you can decide
         for yourself how you feel about it.

If you answered "yes" to any of these questions,
you might want to give a little more thought to the
important choices in your life.

OUTSIDE THE BOX

Have you done things that weren't really you? Do you want to regain your values and go back to the person you were before? Here are some ways to get started:

- <u>Journal</u> about your feelings, where you've been and where you want to go.
- <u>Walk</u> because it does wonders to clear your head.
- <u>Reconnect</u> with old friends, old hobbies and things that bring you back to being the person you used to be.
- <u>Talk</u> with trusted friends or family members about what's going on.

DO YOU KNOW ANY TRENDSETTERS? You know, they're the ones who blaze their own trail by wearing unique clothes or proudly participating in some obscure hobby like gothic croquet. They're the ones who make things cool by the very idea that they're not afraid to be seen as the individuals they are.

Standing up in today's society of conformists and yelling "I just want to be me" isn't easy. It takes a lot of courage and self-confidence. But the great thing about it is that the more you stand up for who you are and speak your truth, the easier it will become.

THE WORD

A **conformist** is someone who adopts styles or habits of other people in order to fit in.

I Just Want to Be Me

You think that they'll always be there
Through it all.
But you can't always rely on them
To catch you when you fall.

Sometimes you find yourself
Lost in the crowd.
Doing all that you can
But never making them proud.

You follow each step
That everyone takes—
You're living your life for them,
But as a fake.

They lie to you,
You lie to them.
When will you realize,
You can do whatever you want to do?

When you finally stand up,
You find yourself pushed back down.
And you're left all alone,
With nothing but a frown.

Nobody cares
About what you have to say,
In this life,
It only goes their way.

CONSIDER THIS . . .

Some people are **natural born leaders**, and people tend to follow their example, while others are more comfortable **following** the lead of others. Which type are **you**?

Nobody cares,
What you want to do.
For they rule everyone,
Including you.

Nobody knows what it's
    like,
To sit at home and be
    alone tonight.
And nobody knows what
    it's like,
To never have anything ever go right.

But young girl, stop your crying,
Stop all your tears.
No one can help you,
You just have to get over your fears.

Stand up to those,
Who put pressure on you.
Let them know what it is
That you want to do.

If they laugh,
Then you laugh, too.
If they point,
Just point back at you.

Let them know you're sick
Of always following them around,
That you don't want to be,
Just another background sound.

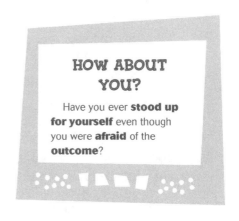

HOW ABOUT YOU?

Have you ever **stood up for yourself** even though you were **afraid** of the **outcome**?

Seen It?

Tom Cruise plays a burned-out sports agent whose life changes for the better when he takes a stand in the movie, *Jerry Maguire* (1996).

You'll feel much better,
After conquering your fear.
But you'll still be looking,
For someone to be near.

Someone will come,
They eventually do.
'Cause after you stood up,
They'll be looking up to you.

Just take a lesson from this.
Never let anyone tell you how to live your life,
Or who you should be.
Just smile and say back to them,
"I just want to be me."

Isabel Thottam, Age 15

WHERE DO YOU STAND?

Do you do things just to fit in?

Everyone in your group of friends has dyed their hair a different color, and you're the only one "au naturale." Do you buy a box of dye and go platinum?

- NO WAY! (0 points)
- MAYBE (1 point)
- YEAH, WHY NOT? (2 points)

All of your friends are on diets and picking at salads at lunchtime. You're not dieting, and furthermore, they're serving your favorite lunch today—meatloaf! Do you skip the meat and grab a salad?

- NO WAY! (0 points)
- MAYBE (1 point)
- YEAH, WHY NOT? (2 points)

Everyone's going to the Death Cab for Cutie concert, but you'd rather go to the symphony with your folks. Do you go see Death Cab so you can talk about the concert at school on Monday along with everyone else?

- NO WAY! (0 points)
- MAYBE (1 point)
- YEAH, WHY NOT? (2 points)

You overhear some serious scoop in the bathroom about another student. You know the info will score you major points among your group of friends. Do you pass along the gossip to show that you're "in the know"?

- NO WAY! (0 points)
- MAYBE (1 point)
- YEAH, WHY NOT? (2 points)

You love your Irish folk dancing classes, but suddenly realize that if your friends knew how you were spending your Saturday mornings, they might think you're a nerd. Do you give up your dance classes to save face?

- NO WAY! (0 points)
- MAYBE (1 point)
- YEAH, WHY NOT? (2 points)

Add up your points:

    0–3 = You feel confident in who you are and don't need to act different for anyone else.

    4–7 = You often feel conflicted over wanting to fit in and trying to march to the beat of your own drum.

    8–10 = Fitting in is the most important thing to you, no matter the cost.

WE'VE SEEN THE THEME IN A MILLION MOVIES. Rich kid with everything that money can buy and a house as big as a museum feels sad and empty inside. Maybe she never sees her parents because they're too wrapped up in their careers, or maybe he has no friends because everyone is intimidated by him. While these movies are somewhat cliché, what I like about them is that the theme reinforces the notion that we *all have our struggles to deal with*. No one is immune. Why then do we so easily forget this when we're busy labeling others as being different from us?

Seen It?

First Daughter (2004) stars Katie Holmes as the classic "poor little rich girl."

Abused

Prep, goth, punk, geek,
Slut, stupid, loser, freak.
Society dictates who we are.
They cause our heartache,
   we're left with scars.
I hate all the labels,
I hate all the names.
All they do is cause suffering
   and pain.

The goth wears black,
Has piercings and tattoos.
But when she goes home,
She gets abused.

For Real?

Today, just about **everything** has a **label**, even people. The use of labels goes back as far as 3,000 B.C., when labels were put on the bottom of pots in China to identify who made them.

She wears all black
To match her bruise.

The prep, she's a cheerleader,
Homecoming queen.
She's got a reputation for being
    mean.
She goes for a ride in her
    boyfriend's car.
Who is he? The football star.
When they go out, she is abused.
She wears the makeup to hide her bruise.

The geeks, they wear glasses,
They feel so alone,
They try to hide in their own little zone.
When they go to school,
They get abused.
Yeah, life sucks.
But what else is new?

We aren't so different, you and me.
You may be a slut,
You may be a freak,
You may be a prep,
You may be a geek,
You may be a goth,
You may be a priss.
None of that matters.
What matters, is
We all need help.

For Real?
1 in 10 boys and girls report being **physically abused** by their girlfriend or boyfriend.

Address Book

If you're in an **abusive relationship** and need help, call the **National Youth Violence Prevention Resource Center's** hotline at **1-866-SAFEYOUTH** (1-866-723-3968) from 8 A.M. to 6 P.M. ET. (1-800-243-7012 is TTY number.) Or go to *www.safeyouth.org*. If you are in danger and need immediate help, always call 911.

We're all the same.
We all get abused.
We all get called names.

Taylor Davis, Age 12

    HAVE YOU EVER HEARD THE SAYING "HINDSIGHT IS 20/20"?
That means that it's easy to look back on our mistakes and say
"Oh, I should have done *this*" or "If only I'd done *that*, things would
be different." (The 20/20 refers to perfect vision.) Well, things
might be different, but then you wouldn't be who you are, either.
That's because we're all the sum of our experiences. They're what
make us uniquely us.
    This next poem, "Lessons to a Former Self," is written by an
author who, as an eighteen-year-old, looked at a picture of herself taken when she was ten. If she could go back and give
her younger self some advice for the rough years ahead, here's
what she would say.

Lessons to a Former Self

Strange to imagine an innocence so unknowing, so intent.
Eager to live your life,
You'd never take it one day at a time,
Preferring to live by experiences,
Rather than by expectations.

Unbeknownst of what is to befall you,
You are content in your youth
And think that wisdom can be learned rather than taught.

I want to warn you of what is to come,
To prepare you for the times that will seem impossible to
    survive.
Because you will be knocked down
And you will feel devastation and defeat.
You will have your heart broken
And you will know betrayal.
You will fall flat on your face
And find yourself without the strength to get up again.
It is at these times that you will learn the purpose of friends;
They will hold you up and teach you to stand again.

I won't lie to you. There will be dark times.
But along with those, you will find joy and happiness.
You will experience life, and you will experience death.
This will be one of the most difficult lessons,
And it will cause you to question the existence of God.
You will find an answer to
    that question.
You will fall in love with a
    boy at sixteen
And two years later you'll
    finally understand that he
    doesn't feel the same.
He will hurt you, but you
    will survive.
You will love again.

HOW ABOUT YOU?

Have you ever **fallen flat
on your face** only to come out
of the situation even stronger
than you were before?

At age seventeen you will be in your
    first car accident.
It will scare you.
That will be a good thing.
You will watch your friends make
    mistakes.
You will join in.
You will lose friends and gain others.
In the end, you'll be the better for it.
You will discover passions
And will learn about sacrifice and dedication.
Sometimes your sacrifices will be rewarded.
Sometimes not.

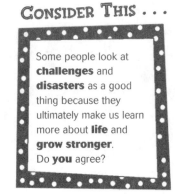

CONSIDER THIS . . .

Some people look at **challenges** and **disasters** as a good thing because they ultimately make us learn more about **life** and **grow stronger**. Do **you** agree?

You will define who you are through your gifts to others.
You don't know what these are right now,
But you'll learn.
You will face disasters.
They will all come at the same time,
And make you want to give up.
They are there to test you.
Get through it, and they will make you stronger—
They're just preparing you for what else is to come.
Most of all, I want to tell you
That you will be okay.
When you're going through rough times, you need to remember:
Just keep going.

                                                    Paige Cerulli, Age 18

OUTSIDE THE BOX

What would you teach your former self if you could go back in time? Try answering these questions in your journal (or any scrap of paper) to realize how far you've come:

- Write about something that you thought was the end of the world that happened to you three or more years ago. If you can't think of anything that huge, then write about a time when you lost your temper or got really upset.
- How do you feel about what happened now?
- What did you end up learning from the experience?
- Would you handle it differently if the same thing happened today?

I'D SOMEHOW MANAGED TO MAKE IT THROUGH my teen years without ever seriously hurting myself—no broken bones, no stitches, no bumps or bruises too intense that they needed any real attention beyond an ice pack and some Mercurochrome. Then came a fateful tennis game one fine May afternoon.

My boyfriend had just hit a nice backhand, sending the ball curving down on my side of the court at a million miles an hour. I lunged to try and get the ball on the bounce and instead somehow managed to step directly on it. If you've never stepped on a ball or other small, moving object before, I highly recommend that you don't. Why? Because when one object (the ball) is moving fast in one direction, and the momentum of the other object (my body) is going in another, things just aren't going to end well.

I collapsed to the ground in a twisted pile, with my ankle, snapped and broken, at the bottom of the heap. My cast-free youth had ended, and I was crutch-bound for the next three months.

When the cast finally did come off, my doctor gave me a bunch of exercises to do to strengthen the tendons and ligaments around the ankle, and told me that I could gently start running in another month, which I did. But even after a few months, I found myself running very gingerly, afraid that my ankle would roll once again under the weight of my body. Finally, I called my doctor and talked with him about my concerns. Imagine my surprise when he said that, while my ankle might feel weak for a while, one thing I didn't have to worry about was breaking the ankle in the same place ever again. In fact, it's nearly impossible to break the same bone in the same place twice, because when the fracture heals, it becomes even stronger than before. This next poem, "The Broken Vase," cleverly reflects the same sentiment.

The Broken Vase

There once was a vase
On a shelf in a room
Kept there by a girl,
It was a family heirloom.

The girl loved her vase,
Kept it spotlessly clean
And it stood on her shelf
Until she was fourteen.

Then her life got confusing,
Everything fell apart,
And though her fears were
   not voiced,
They were felt in her heart.

Then one night after school
As she looked at the vase
She felt an ugly look
Come down over her face.

HOW ABOUT YOU?

Have you ever **destroyed** something in an **emotional outburst** and regretted it later?

"I hate you!" she shouted
As she picked up the jar
And hurled it through the air—
It didn't fly far.

With an earsplitting crash,
The old vase hit the door
And split down the center
As it fell to the floor.

Her brief rage now over,
She saw what she'd done
And tears flooding her cheeks,
Crossed the room at a run.

She realized too late
What she'd done had been wrong;
It wasn't the vase that she'd hated,
But herself all along.

She'd smashed something
  precious
Because she was stressed.
But how could she fix it?
She'd just try her best.

And so, armed with a glue gun,
She toiled by night
To mend the old vase
And put matters right.

When the next morning came,
The girl looked at the vase
And a smile appeared
Upon her tired face.

It was no longer perfect,
No need to pretend,
But now, stronger than ever,
It would last 'til the end.

Ashley Yang, Age 16

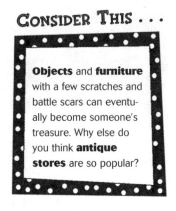

CONSIDER THIS . . .

Objects and **furniture** with a few scratches and battle scars can eventually become someone's treasure. Why else do you think **antique stores** are so popular?

Take the Quiz:
DO YOU KNOW HOW TO USE YOUR VOICE

1. This girl you've known since kindergarten has been the target of verbal bullying for as long as you can remember. When you were younger, you didn't think much of it, but now that you're older, you are constantly shocked at the abuse this poor girl still takes. What do you do?

   ___ A. You don't do anything about it, other than try to avoid situations where the girl is being made fun of in front of you. What difference could you possibly make when you consider how long this has been going on?

   ___ B. You know that all it takes is one person to take a stand, and so you do just that. You've got enough sway at your school that if people realize you don't think it's cool, hopefully they'll follow your lead and back off.

   ___ C. You don't say anything to your friends, but when you have a chance, you talk with the girl and try to befriend her, giving her suggestions about how to deal with the verbal abuse and avoid situations where it might happen.

2. You've just started working at the local movie theater, and you love your job until you realize that one of the managers is harassing some of the girls on staff. How do you handle it?

   ___ A. You report the manager's behavior to his boss and do your best to ensure it doesn't happen while you're on duty.

   ___ B. You don't think that the manager is behaving very professionally, but since this is your first job, you're not sure if this kind of thing is normal. You don't approve, but you decide to try and protect the girls who are being targeted.

_____ C. You ignore it. Why bother risking your cool new job for people you barely even know?

3. The new principal at your school has just enforced a policy that says the school newspaper content has to be approved by her before it can go to publication. You've been on staff for three years and are finally editorial director of the paper, and you couldn't be more upset about the new rule. What do you do?

_____ A. You think the rule is wrong, but you don't want to do anything to jeopardize your standing with the paper. You were counting on this position to help you get into college with a writing scholarship.

_____ B. You go along with the principal's request, but publish an editorial in the paper stating your objections to the new rule and suggesting the student body take a stand against the regulation.

_____ C. You meet with the paper advisor and talk about what recourse you have, questioning the rule as being a form of censorship. You launch a local media campaign to try and put pressure on the principal to back down from her stance.

4. Your biology teacher split the class into groups at the beginning of the year, and you've been meeting weekly with the same group of girls for months now. You've become close enough friends to realize that something is wrong when one of the girls starts coming to meetings with bruises on her body. What do you do?

_____ A. You approach the girl after school and ask her if everything's okay. You offer to listen if she'd like to talk, and let her know that if she needs help with a situation in her home life, that you'll be there every step of the way.

_____ B. Unless the girl comes to you for help, you don't feel like it's your place to say anything. If she were really in jeopardy from abuse at home, you figure she'd tell an adult who could help her.

_____ C. You talk with the other girls in your group about your suspicions and get their thoughts. You decide to wait to see if the bruises continue before taking a next step.

5. A teacher in your school breaks up a fight between two boys—one white and one Hispanic. You notice that he treats the Hispanic student more roughly than the other student, and even mutters an ethnic slur under his breath as he drags both students to the principal's office. Which of these is most like something you'd do?

___ A. You are upset and tell your friends what happened, asking their advice on what to do about it. Eventually, you just let it drop, but you vow to stand up to such injustices if it ever happens again.

___ B. You are outraged at this clear demonstration of racial injustice, and you aren't about to let it slide. You insist on meeting with the principal to give your version of the story, and threaten to write a letter to the school board if the teacher in question isn't disciplined.

___ C. Even though you saw what happened, you'd rather not get involved. You're sure this kind of thing happens all the time, so what difference would it make if you stuck your nose in other people's business?

So, do you know how to speak up and use your voice when it counts? Give yourself the following points:

1. a = 30, b = 10, c = 20; 2. a = 10, b = 20, c = 30; 3. a = 30, b = 20, c = 10; 4. a = 10, b = 30, c = 20; 5. a = 20, b = 10, c = 30.

50–70 points = Grab a megaphone and let it blare! You are passionate about your ideas and you're not afraid to speak your mind. You know that you've got power in your words and actions, and you exercise that power whenever you have a chance.

80–120 points = You feel inspired to take a stand, but don't quite know how to go about it. Try being more proactive when you can. If you find yourself suppressing an urge to speak up about something, that's the time to do exactly that.

130–150 points = For whatever reason, you haven't yet discovered how good it feels to speak up about something you feel strongly about. Try speaking up in a safe environment, like in a class with a supportive teacher, and see how it feels. When you realize that people listen to what you have to say, you'll find that using your voice is the most empowering thing you can do.

EPILOGUE

THIS MAY BE the end of the book, but we know that you will continue to face challenges in your lives every day—whether it's struggling to be comfortable in your own skin, trying to find a place to fit in at home or at school, or coming to terms with a painful loss. And while this book doesn't offer "quick fixes," we hope that through reading the stories and material in this book, you will discover ways for getting through difficult times yourself, and above all, know that you're not alone. We all experience pain and heartache, we all struggle to figure out who are . . . it's what makes us human and gives us perspective so that we can grow and learn and do amazing things with our lives. Lean on this book like you would a good friend, and whenever you feel like no one gets what you're going through, flip it open and read a story . . . knowing others have gotten through their challenges just might be the inspiration you need to get through yours.

SUPPORTING OTHERS

YOUTHNOISE (*www.youthnoise.com*) is a collection of youth—from all 50 states, and more than 176 countries—who banned together with a small group of adults working to provide information from more than 300 non-profit partners that will spark youth action and voice.

The mission of YouthNOISE is to enable young people to become informed, engaged and connected citizens with a voice that communicates around the world. Teens use the more than 2,000 pages of content and tools on the YN Web site to find inspiration and resources to catalyze and deepen their volunteerism, philanthropy, social entrepreneurship and advocacy in their local and global communities. YN also serves as a sounding board, a "place" where teens voice their civic ideas, opinions, concerns and solutions to policymakers and the press to influence issues affecting their generation, and connect to a community of fellow youth to share ideas, inspiration and best practices.

YouthNOISE is not only enticing teens to help, they're showing them how. In helping young people connect their passions to the community processes that make change happen— volunteerism, philanthropy and active civic participation (i.e., voting, lobbying)—YouthNOISE hopes to motivate them to use their civic rights and exercise and participate in civic life. The site enables teens to learn more about the issues important to their lives—body image, poverty, war, employment, AIDS, sustainable farming, gender preference, voting. YN supports teens' willingness and desire to respect differences born of socioeconomic, geographic and cultural circumstance.

YouthNOISE currently serves approximately 750,000 teens visiting the Web site monthly made up mostly of mainstream youth, 13 to 24 years old, but primarily high-school aged, from all nations and all walks of life passionate about something, but unsure how to connect. On the YN site, a common denominator is a desire to find a role in building a better world. More than 90 percent of the Web site's content is written by youth. A team of 150 writing interns, working virtually from around the globe, creates the bulk of new content for the site. They write about their personal experiences and opinions. One editor manages this team, leaving the individual voices of the writers intact and allowing YN to be a true medium for teen self-expression on serious topics that impact civic life. At least two new articles are posted to the site each day and generated by users.

YouthNOISE has received a number of awards for its efforts to engage youth, including the Cable and Wireless Childnet Award in the nonprofit category (2003), the People's Choice Award in 2003, as well as the Golden Globe Award for Technical Excellence.

Speak out. Take action. MAKE SOME NOISE!

For more information, contact:

YouthNOISE

1255 Post Street, Suite 1120, San Francisco, CA 94109

E-mail: *help@youthnoise.com*, Web site: *www.youthnoise.com*

Who Is JACK CANFIELD?

Jack Canfield is one of America's leading experts in the development of human potential and personal effectiveness. He is both a dynamic, entertaining speaker and a highly sought-after trainer. Jack has a wonderful ability to inform and inspire audiences toward increased levels of self-esteem and peak performance. Jack most recently released a book for success entitled *The Success Principles: How to Get from Where You Are to Where You Want to Be.*

He is the author and narrator of several bestselling audio- and videocassette programs, including *Self-Esteem and Peak Performance, How to Build High Self-Esteem, Self-Esteem in the Classroom* and *Chicken Soup for the Soul—Live.* He is regularly seen on television shows such as *Good Morning America, 20/20* and *NBC Nightly News.* Jack has coauthored numerous books, including the *Chicken Soup for the Soul* series, *Dare to Win* and *The Aladdin Factor* (all with Mark Victor Hansen), *100 Ways to Build Self-Concept in the Classroom* (with Harold C. Wells), *Heart at Work* (with Jacqueline Miller), and *The Power of Focus* (with Les Hewitt and Mark Victor Hansen).

Jack is a regularly featured speaker for professional associations, school districts, government agencies, churches, hospitals, sales organizations and corporations. His clients have included the American Dental Association, the American Management Association, AT&T, Campbell's Soup, Clairol, Domino's Pizza, GE, Hartford Insurance, ITT, Johnson & Johnson, the Million Dollar Roundtable, NCR, New England Telephone, Re/Max, Scott Paper, TRW and Virgin Records. Jack has taught on the faculty of Income Builders International, a school for entrepreneurs.

Jack conducts an annual seven-day training called Breakthrough to Success. It attracts entrepreneurs, educators, counselors, parenting trainers, corporate trainers, professsional speakers, ministers and others interested in improving their lives and the lives of others.

For free gifts from Jack and information on all his material and availability go to:

www.jackcanfield.com
Self-Esteem Seminars
P.O. Box 30880
Santa Barbara, CA 93130
phone: 805-563-2935 • fax: 805-563-2945

Who Is MARK VICTOR HANSEN?

In the area of human potential, no one is better known and more respected than Mark Victor Hansen. For more than thirty years, Mark has focused solely on helping people from all walks of life reshape their personal vision of what's possible. His powerful messages of possibility, opportunity and action have helped create startling and powerful change in thousands of organizations and millions of individuals worldwide.

He is a prolific writer with many bestselling books such as *The One Minute Millionaire, The Power of Focus, The Aladdin Factor* and *Dare to Win*, in addition to the *Chicken Soup for the Soul* series.

Mark is also the founder of MEGA Book Marketing University and Building Your MEGA Speaking Empire. Both are annual conferences where Mark coaches and teaches new and aspiring authors, speakers and experts on building lucrative publishing and speaking careers.

His energy and exuberance travel still further through mediums such as television (*Oprah, CNN* and *The Today Show*), print (*Time, U.S. News & World Report, USA Today, New York Times* and *Entrepreneur*) and countless radio and newspaper interviews as he assures our planet's people that "You can easily create the life you deserve."

As a philanthropist and humanitarian, Mark works tirelessly for organizations such as Habitat for Humanity, American Red Cross, March of Dimes, Childhelp USA and many others. He is the recipient of numerous awards that honor his entrepreneurial spirit, philanthropic heart and business acumen, including the prestigious Horatio Alger Award for his extraordinary life achievements.

Mark Victor Hansen is an enthusiastic crusader of what's possible and is driven to make the world a better place.

www.markvictorhansen.com
Mark Victor Hansen & Associates, Inc.
P.O. Box 7665
Newport Beach, CA 92658
phone: 949-764-2640 • fax: 949-722-6912

Who Is DEBORAH REBER?

Deborah is a former children's television executive who now writes for teens and tweens, most recently coauthoring *Chicken Soup for the Teenage Soul's The Real Deal: School* and *The Real Deal: Friends*. Deborah is the coeditor and copublisher of *Bold Ink: Collected Voices of Women and Girls*, an anthology by WriteGirl, a nonprofit creative-writing organization that matches women writers with teen girls for one-on-one mentoring. She currently sits on WriteGirl's Board of Advisors. Deborah's first nonfiction book, *Run for Your Life: A Book for Beginning Women Runners*, is a self-help book with the goal of making the sport of running accessible to women of all abilities.

Prior to becoming a fulltime writer, Deborah worked in children's television, developing original programming for Cartoon Network, managing ancillary projects for *Blue's Clues* (Nickelodeon), and producing an animation international campaign about children's rights for UNICEF. While at *Blue's Clues*, she wrote more than a dozen *Blue's Clues* books, including two *New York Times* bestsellers, and coauthored a line of educational workbooks. She has produced several documentaries, including *Drawing Insight* and *Seven Days in Somalia*, and consults with companies like Nickelodeon, Disney Channel, McGraw-Hill and Offramp Films.

Deborah leads writing and creative workshops for teens, most recently participating in Mind on the Media's annual conference, Turn Beauty Inside Out. She has an M.A. in Media Studies from the New School for Social Research in New York City (1996), and a B.A. in Broadcast Journalism from the Pennsylvania State University (1991). She lives in Seattle with her husband Derin, son Asher and their dog Baxter, where she enjoys running, hiking and gardening. To contact Deborah, write or e-mail her at:

The Real Deal
4509 Interlake Avenue North, #281
Seattle, WA 98103
E-mail: *submissions@deborahreber.com*
Web Site: *www.deborahreber.com*

CONTRIBUTORS

Dani Allred is a resident of North Ogden, Utah. She will be graduating from high school this spring. She enjoys music and writing, and is involved in her school and community. She believes you should be glad about life, for it gives you a chance to love, to work, to play and to look at the stars.

Terry Beasley is a student at Binghamton University where she plans to major in creative writing with a minor in higher education. Please e-mail her at *terryrosebeasley@rcn.com*.

Sarah Boesing is a high-school student. When she isn't writing or attending school or church, she enjoys reading, acting, service projects, playing softball and learning to play the guitar.

Tally Bower is a writer, painter and boss DJ. He plans on studying architecture and sustainable design in college. He is distressed about the current state of global affairs and feels awkward that people are spending time reading about his insignifigant troubles when there are so many pressing issues at hand.

Neda Bowren is a Senior in high school and has a passion for writing. She plans to attend college to major in Business/Creative writing. After college, she would like to move to a larger city and focus on becoming an author. Neda can be reached via e-mail at *neda bowren@hotmail.com*.

Ian Brown studied writing at a small art high school in North Charleston and enjoys surfing, poetry and music. Ian received a national scholastic writing award for a fictional short story and is currently getting his second poem published.

Paige Cerulli is currently a college student working toward a degree in music performance. She enjoys horseback riding, writing poetry and playing the flute. She would like to thank the many teachers who encouraged her writing and told her to "keep at it." Please e-mail her at *PoetryNMotion@mymailstation.com*.

Maurisa Cohen is currently an undergraduate student at the University of Western Ontario. She hopes to become a lawyer. Please e-mail her at *ashaaley@hotmail.com*.

Shelby Coleman is a student at UH in Johnson City, Tennessee. She enjoys listening to music, writing poetry, reading, soccer, rock-climbing and hanging out with her friends.

Jane Concha is currently a sophomore at Loretto Academy High School in El Paso, Texas. She enjoys reading and writing and wants to continue, whether it be a profession or a hobby. Please e-mail her at *sailorQ1@hotmail.com*.

Taylor Davis is a middle-school student in South Carolina. She enjoys participating in sports such as softball and basketball. She also enjoys writing short stories and poems that people her age can relate to. Taylor is currently involved in theater classes and the local Christian Youth Theater Program.

Claire Deden is in tenth grade at Red Wing High School. She hopes to pursue a career in acting. She enjoys being with her friends, dancing, reading and promoting a healthy body image through her "Go Girls" involvement. She plans to write an autobiography about her struggle with anorexia.

Jessica Ekstrom is a ninth-grade student in Charlotte, North Carolina. She enjoys volleyball, basketball, surfing and hanging out with friends. Jessica hopes to one day coach a team. In her spare time, she likes to write poetry to express how she feels about certain issues.

Mary Elizabeth Elsey graduated from Green High School with honors in 2005. She is currently studying at Ohio Northern University with a double major in Theater and English Arts Education. Mary hopes to either become a high-school teacher or a college professor. Please feel free to e-mail Mary at *m-elsey@onu.edu*.

Ashley Flynn is a high-school student in Ontario, Canada. She has a passion for writing and is currently a member of her school newspaper. In her spare time, Ashley loves to dance and is very family oriented. When she wrote this poem, she was thirteen years old and often wrote to express her feelings.

Allyssa Gleason is president of her senior class in Redding, California. She enjoys reading, writing, bowling and waterskiing. Next year, she plans to go to a college in the Napa Valley and major in English.

Jasmine Highsmith is a part of the class of 2006 at South Central High School in North Carolina. She's written over fifty poems and is most famous for her poem "I'm No Longer Mad," which has been published in the *International Book of Poetry*. She loves to write and plans to become a journalist. Please e-mail her at *JasmineHigh smith@yahoo.com*.

Lyssa Hoganson enjoys reading, writing and drawing. Her two cats constantly find her open book to be the perfect napping place. She and her friends write and illustrate a comic strip entitled "Learning to Think." You can e-mail her at *blackcatgurl@aol.com*.

Paulina Karpis is a student at Stuyvesant High School in New York. She enjoys dancing ballet, playing the piano, reading and writing.

MacKenzie Mantrom is from a small town. She wrote this story because her friend passed away, and it was very hard for Mackenzie to get over the loss. Having this story published has helped her to overcome her grief, and Mackenzie's story is dedicated to the loving memory of her friend.

Eri Mizobe wrote her story when she was thirteen-years-old. She is a Hawaiian-born, Japanese-Cantonese girl, and enjoys reading, writing and studying. Her goal is to become an author some day. When you read her story, she hopes you will find comfort and happiness. E-mail her at *eriballerina@hotmail.com*.

Galit Oren plans to major in English with a Creative Writing emphasis. She organized and held a teen poetry slam through her high-school senior project. Galit hopes to inspire others and help fight illiteracy. She enjoys reading. Galit is an active member of Redmond's Association of Spokenword in Redmond, Washington.

John Penny was born in Oxnard, California in 1986. His favorite holidays are Christmas and Easter. John enjoys studying meteorolgy and spending time with his family who lives in Worcester, Massachusetts. He plans on pursuing a career in modeling and being an inventor.

Gabrielle Phan, 14 years old, attends Valley View Middle School in Minnesota, and will soon be going to John F. Kennedy High School. She believes that the world should learn sign language due to speech impairments. She also loves to study biology and astrology. In her spare time she writes short stories and poems. She loves her family and friends dearly and she is currently in love with an incredible guy named Joel.

Andrea Popp recently graduated from Crown Point High School and plans to attend a local college, where she will major in Education. She dreams of being a bestselling author and is currently working on her first novel. Please e-mail her at *hot_popp13@msn.com*.

Joanne Qiao is a student at Niskayuna High School and is an involved staff member of the school newspaper. She enjoys synchronized swimming and dancing. In the future, Joanne hopes to either be a doctor or a psychologist.

Teresa Rankin hails from Thief River Falls, Minnesota. She is attending Bemidji State University in Minnesota to earn her degree in Theater, and plans to continue with her education to earn her Master's Degree and possibly a Doctorate in the same field. Teresa enjoys all aspects of the theater, particularly musicals and movies, music, photography, and writing both poetry and prose. You may contact her at *mizmouse86@hotmail.com*.

Brooke Raphalian is fourteen years old and is in the eighth grade. She lives in New Jersey with her parents and her dog, Freckles. Brooke enjoys writing, shopping, playing tennis and being with her friends.

Liia Rudolph is a senior at Strath Haven High School, and she loves to write, act, sing, and babysit for fabulous kids. She believes in people and the magic of words. If you'd like to contact her, her e-mail is *littleguccidress@gmail.com*. She'd especially like to thank Mrs. Farrell for all her faith.

Sarah Sacco will be attending Arizona State University to study Journalism and Mass Communication. She enjoys reading and writing contemporary fiction, listening to music, studying spirituality, researching local history and pondering the meaning of life.

Kaylee Stark graduated from J.W. Mitchell High School in New Port Richey, Florida, in May 2006. She was co-editor-in-chief of the award-winning *Stampede Yearbook*. Kaylee plans to attend college where she will study journalism. Contact her at *koolkatkay69@ aol.com*.

Heather Steadman is fifteen years old and in the tenth grade. She has been writing short stories and poetry for about five years. Her hobbies are singing, acting, skiing, cooking and baby-sitting. Heather hopes to become a forensic specialist.

Lucille Taquet was born in Paris, France, and boasts both French and American nationalities. She is in the Anglophone International section in her French public middle school. Lucille enjoys reading, singing and riding. She goes to the United States yearly where she enjoys being American and seeing her family.

Isabel Thottam is currently a freshman at Central Catholic High School. She plays varsity tennis for her school and hopes to play professionally in her future. Isabel enjoys traveling around the world to places such as Spain, Italy and France. Her favorite TV shows are *Lost*, and *The O.C.*.

Mallory Ward is an honor student currently attending Conner High School, where she enjoys cheerleading, cross country and track. Mallory enjoys writing and has a great passion for theater. She has performed in several theatrical productions, including performances with Jenny Wiley Theatre and Cincinnati Young People Theatre.

Katelynn Wilton is a junior who lives with her mom, dad, brother and two cocker spaniels. Her past credits include winning a contest from *National Geographic* and the United States Mint, being published in *Chicken Soup: The Real Deal: School* and various smaller awards.

Ashley Yang is a junior in high school and enjoys reading, writing, participating in Model United Nations club and being with her friends. She hopes to be a teacher some day and extends her gratitude to those who have helped her through tough times.

PERMISSIONS

Silent Scream. Reprinted by permission of Ashley Mie Yang and Jean Pauk. ©2005 Ashley Mie Yang.

Left Behind. Reprinted by permission of Maurisa Cohen. ©2005 Maurisa Cohen.

Saying Good-Bye to Fairy Tales. Reprinted by permission of Andrea Maria Popp and Rita Maria Popp ©2005 Andrea Maria Popp.

Thin Ice. Reprinted by permission of Teresa Joy Rankin. ©2002 Teresa Joy Rankin.

Living with Scoliosis. Reprinted by permission of Galit Oren. ©2005 Galit Oren.

Makeup. Reprinted by permission of Ashley Flynn and Lori-Ellen Flynn. ©2005 Ashley Flynn.

The Meeting. Reprinted by permission of Ashley Mie Yang and Jean Pauk. ©2005 Ashley Mie Yang.

Anorexia. Reprinted by permission of Claire Marie Deden and Deborah Ann Deden. ©2004 Claire Marie Deden.

Handing Over my Life. Reprinted by permission of Joanne Qioa and Ying Wang. ©2005 Joanne Qioa.

One Cut. Reprinted by permission of Taylor Johnston Davis and Julie Davis. ©2004 Taylor Johnston Davis.

NOTES

NOTES

MORE IN THE SERIES

Code #2556 • $14.95

Code #317X • $14.95

COLLECT THEM ALL